Software Reading Techniques

Twenty Techniques for More Effective Software Review and Inspection

Yang-Ming Zhu

Apress®

Software Reading Techniques: Twenty Techniques for More Effective Software Review and Inspection

Yang-Ming Zhu
Solon, Ohio
USA

ISBN-13 (pbk): 978-1-4842-2345-1   ISBN-13 (electronic): 978-1-4842-2346-8
DOI 10.1007/978-1-4842-2346-8

Library of Congress Control Number: 2016959789

Managing Director: Welmoed Spahr
Acquisitions Editor: Robert Hutchinson
Developmental Editor: Laura Berendson
Technical Reviewer: Weidong Liao
Editorial Board: Steve Anglin, Pramila Balen, Laura Berendson, Aaron Black,
    Louise Corrigan, Jonathan Gennick, Robert Hutchinson, Celestin Suresh John,
    Nikhil Karkal, James Markham, Susan McDermott, Matthew Moodie, Natalie Pao,
    Gwenan Spearing
Coordinating Editor: Rita Fernando
Copy Editor: Angela Warner
Compositor: SPi Global
Indexer: SPi Global
Cover Image: Designed by Pio_pio - Freepik.com

Distributed to the book trade worldwide by Springer Science+Business Media New York, 233 Spring Street, 6th Floor, New York, NY 10013. Phone 1-800-SPRINGER, fax (201) 348-4505, e-mail orders-ny@springer-sbm.com, or visit www.springeronline.com. Apress Media, LLC is a California LLC and the sole member (owner) is Springer Science + Business Media Finance Inc (SSBM Finance Inc). SSBM Finance Inc is a Delaware corporation.

For information on translations, please e-mail rights@apress.com, or visit www.apress.com.

Apress and friends of ED books may be purchased in bulk for academic, corporate, or promotional use. eBook versions and licenses are also available for most titles. For more information, reference our Special Bulk Sales–eBook Licensing web page at www.apress.com/bulk-sales.

Any source code or other supplementary materials referenced by the author in this text is available to readers at www.apress.com. For detailed information about how to locate your book's source code, go to www.apress.com/source-code/.

Printed on acid-free paper

To Xiao-Hong, Harold, Alex, and the rest of my family.

Contents at a Glance

Contents

About the Author

Yang-Ming Zhu is a Principal Scientist at Philips Healthcare, currently serving as the software architect for the Recon and Imaging Physics team for Advanced Molecular Imaging. He practices and researches image processing and software engineering with a focus on software architecture, requirements engineering, best practices, software quality, and processes. He is a senior member of IEEE and has published more than 80 book chapters and papers in such journals as IEEE Software, IT Professional, IEEE Trans Medical Imaging, IEEE Trans Image Processing, IEEE Trans Signal Processing, Journal of Nuclear Medicine, Physical Review Letters, and Applied Physical Letters. He holds nine U.S. patents (additional seven are pending approval), the Software Architecture Professional Certificate from the Software Engineering Institute at Carnegie Mellon University, and advanced degrees in computer science (MS from Kent State University), biomedical engineering (MS/BS from Shanghai Jiaotong University), and bioelectronics (PhD from Southeast University).

About the Technical Reviewer

Dr.Weidong Liao is currently an associate Professor at Shepherd University, Shepherdstown, West Virginia. Dr. Liao received his Masters and Ph.D. degrees in Computer Science from Kent State University and had software development experience in Microsoft Corporation and other companies. Dr. Liao made his major research contributions in Internet Accessible Mathematical Computation (IAMC) Application Framework, Internet and Distributed Computing, and Distributed Database System, with numerous publications in these fields. He has also participated in the review process of many conference articles and journal papers in computing areas.

Acknowledgments

The idea of this book was inspired by Kollanus and Koskinen's article, Survey of Software Inspection Research, and based on my presentation to colleagues at Philips on code reading techniques. I thank the researchers and practitioners in the software review/inspection community, who created and validated many software reading techniques upon which the book is based.

Many thanks to Acquisitions Editor Robert Hutchinson, who bestowed trust on me and answered many questions a first-time book author might have; to Developmental Editor Laura Berendson, who edited the book and provided guidance on writing; to Coordinating Editor Rita Fernando, who designed the book cover and made sure I would be on schedule; to Technical Reviewer Professor Weidong Liao, who made sure the book contents are technically sound; and to the rest of the Apress team who supported the project behind the scenes. I would also like to thank Harold Zhu, who improved the presentation in Chapters 1, 3, 5, and 7, and Kevin Wang, who provided suggestions to improve the language in Chapters 2 and 6. Any remaining errors are mine, however. I am profoundly grateful to my mentor Steve Cochoff at Philips for his guidance and friendship for the past almost 20 years.

Most of all I want to thank my wife, Xiao-Hong, and two wonderful boys, Harold and Alex, for letting me disappear at nights and over weekends to research for and write this book. Harold also helped me track down many of the original papers on reading techniques. I am not certain the joy in seeing this book finally published can entirely compensate for the lost family time together.

—Yang-Ming Zhu
Solon, Ohio, September 2016

Introduction

There are many best practices in the software development arena, and there is no other practice as prominent as software review or inspection that has enjoyed the universal agreement on its effectiveness (it finds many defects), efficiency (it finds defects at a low cost), and practicality (it is easy to carry out).

Ever since Fagan published his seminal Fagan Inspection in 1976, software review or inspection has evolved in many aspects. Now the whole industry favors a lightweight, tool-assisted method. Nevertheless, the core of the software review remains the same, i.e., the software review is predominantly an individual reading and analysis activity, since many issues are observed during an individual's preparation phase. The individual reader's skill, training, and expertise play a significant role during reading and analysis and determine the success or failure of software review or inspection. In practice, a wide difference in individual's effectiveness is reported, often as big as 10 times.

As software development professionals, we are trained to write software artifacts such as requirements specifications, design diagrams and descriptions, code modules, test cases, or user interface mockups. We are not trained to read and analyze the documents written by peers, however. To increase an individual's capacity during software review or inspection, reading strategies and proven practices are packaged as reading techniques. This book is designed to promote and disseminate proven reading techniques for professional training and industrial adoption.

There are many reading techniques. To navigate them, the book first discusses basic and more advanced techniques that are applicable to many, if not all, software artifacts, then introduces techniques specially designed for requirements specifications, designs, and code modules. We hope this framework will support your roadmap to adopt the reading techniques in your organization or project.

The author enjoyed researching and writing the book. He certainly hopes you will enjoy reading it and most importantly benefit from adopting these reading techniques in your own practices.

CHAPTER 1

■ ■ ■

Introduction

Software has become an indispensable part of our daily lives, as our dependence on software is constantly increasing. Software fails, and these failures cost money, time, resources, and sometimes even lives. An organization's reputation and success depends on its ability to create and deliver high-quality software. Software quality is thus critically important. This chapter introduces the concept of software quality assurance, discusses software inspection (the most frequently performed software quality assurance activity other than testing), and outlines the contents of this book.

1.1 Software Quality, Software Reviews and Inspections

The software creation process requires a lot of manpower, from requirements and design to implementation and testing. As human beings, we all make mistakes, which are manifested as defects or bugs in software products. Software development is a complex process and tools are frequently used to assist development. People's familiarity with tools and their interaction with tools are the other complicating factors that can potentially inject defects into software products. The nontrivial software product development nowadays may involve many people and teams across the globe. Coordinating the distributed team members and tasks remains a management challenge. Despite many years of software engineering efforts, we are still unable to deliver defect-free software products to the end users. Software defects seem to be inevitable.

Software quality assurance is a structured approach to improve software quality and involves defect prevention, detection and removal, and defect containment activities. Defect detection and removal is mostly emphasized in industry practice, particularly in non-safety critical systems. If it is hard or impossible not to inject defects into software, the next best thing to do is to remove them before they reach end users. It is highly desirable to detect and remove defects as soon as they are injected into software, since defects can be several times more expensive to fix at latter stages of a software project. The escaped or residual defects in field deployment may cause interruption to the user's normal operations, resulting in substantial costs including reduced productivity, data loss or corruption, security vulnerabilities, or even physical harm.

© Yang-Ming Zhu 2016
Y.-M. Zhu, *Software Reading Techniques*, DOI 10.1007/978-1-4842-2346-8_1

Testing and inspection are the two most effective and commonly used methods to detect defects in software. In software testing, a tester runs a software system or its components, executes its functions, observes system behaviors or responses, and determines if the system behaviors conform to its requirements, specifications, or expectations. To test software, one needs a running executable, which is not feasible all the time, particularly for artifacts rather than code. The effectiveness of testing also depends on test cases, and if there is no test case to exercise a particular path of the code, there is no way to tell if there is a defect in that path or not. Dijkstra once famously said that testing can only confirm the presence of a defect, not the absence of a defect (https://en.wikiquote.org/wiki/Edsger_W_Dijkstra).

There are many other quality assurance alternatives besides testing. Software review or inspection is one of these alternatives that is widely practiced. The terms "software review" and "software inspection" are not used consistently in literature. IEEE Standard 1028 defines five types of software reviews: management reviews, technical reviews, inspections, walkthroughs, and audits (IEEE 1028); it treats software inspection as a type of software review. In general software engineering literature, inspection is specific and has a defined process, and review is a more general term. We will use these two terms interchangeably in this book.

Software inspection is a formalized peer review process applicable to any software artifact. It is a static analysis method and was first introduced by Fagan based on his practical experience at IBM in the 1970's (Fagan, 1976). Fagan inspection has been influential ever since it was published. In fact, the IEEE Standard 1028 is largely based on Fagan inspection.

Based on decades of research and industry practices, it is widely established that software inspection is effective (it finds many defects), efficient (low cost per defect), and practical (easy to carry out). We will review the status of software review and inspection in Chapter 2. It has been reported that inspection can detect (and correct) 20% to 90% of defects (Gilb & Graham, 1993, Laitenberger, 2002). The benefits and cost-effectiveness of software inspection have long been recognized. Doolan (1992) reported that every hour invested in inspection has a payback of 30 hours and Russell (1991) claimed that in his organization, every inspection hour saved 33 hours of maintenance work. Although the earlier benefits might be overstated (Porter et al., 1996; Laitenberger, 2002), more recent simulation results have revealed that code inspection saves 39% of defect costs compared to testing alone, and design inspection saves 44% of defect costs compared to testing alone (Briand et al.,1998). Software inspection nowadays is easy to conduct. Books have been published about it (e.g., Gilb, 1993) and standards on review procedures are also available (e.g., IEEE 1028).

During software development, many documents are generated by humans, e.g., requirements specifications, design, code, test plans, test cases, and user documentation. If these documents are used to guide subsequent activities, any errors in these documents may propagate to the downstream activities and artifacts. It is critical to catch and fix errors early to prevent them from propagating down the stream. It is much cheaper for the development organization to fix an error when it is introduced. It is believed that, in general, it would be 10 times more expensive to fix an error if it slips to the next phase. Defects in the released product may result in substantial costs to end users as well.

Table 1-1 shows the cost of fixing a defect depending on when the defect is injected into the software and when the defect is fixed (McConnell, 2004). The first column shows when the defect is injected and the first row shows when the defect is fixed. It assumes the cost to fix the defect injected in the same development phase is 1x. Although the real cost varies and depends on the project size and industry, the general trend is clear.

Requirements, design, and other non-executable artifacts cannot be tested by machines and have to be reviewed by humans. Requirements not implemented yet cannot be machine tested but can be analyzed by humans to see if they meet user needs. Design, particularly early design sketches, can be abstract, imprecise, and incomplete. It is not possible to test designs by machine. With inspection, both requirements and design can be read and analyzed, which does not require the artifacts to be complete or executable. Even for program code, which can be machine-tested, testing and inspection are complementary and uncover different kinds of issues (Basili & Selby, 1987; Juristo & Vegas, 2003). Issues hard to uncover via testing often can be detected by inspection relatively easily. Mantyla and Lassenius (2009) affirmed that code reviews are a good tool for detecting code evolvability defects (documentation, visual representation, and structure) that cannot be found in later phase testing, since the defects do not affect the software's visible functionality. Inspection can be applied to test plan and test cases as well, which further improves the defect detection efficiency of testing.

Table 1-1. *The Cost of Fixing a Defect (adapted from McConnell, 2004)*

	Requirements	Design	Coding	Testing	Deployment
Requirements	1x	3x	5-10x	10x	10-100x
Design	-	1x	10x	15x	25-100x
Coding	-	-	1x	10x	10-25x

The immediate benefit of software review is to detect and fix errors or problems in software artifacts. As a side effect of inspection, the software artifacts become more readable and maintainable. There are other derived benefits to individuals who participate in the review and to the organization as a whole. The author who created the artifacts can use the review outcome as a learning instrument, e.g., he can avoid similar errors in his future work. To other participants, they can also learn from another person's mistakes, particularly if they did not catch the mistakes in their own reviews. The software review can be used to cross-train team members and build a stronger team. Inspection enables a team to share technical expertise. To the organization, fewer mistakes lead to higher quality and better customer satisfaction and less rework and higher development productivity.

If the organization builds a knowledge database of past errors and problems uncovered during software inspection, they can use it to their competitive advantage. In the case of code review, one can identify the most error-prone modules and decide whether redesign or recoding is worthwhile. Certainly more review and more testing in those problematic areas are warranted before the software is released. The organization can also look at the distribution of error types via the Pareto chart and perform root cause analysis of the most common errors. For common systematic errors, the organization can then decide if additional training, better tooling, or an improved development process could help.

1.2   About This Book

In Fagan's inspection and its derivatives, individuals typically read software artifacts, then come together to discuss their findings and hopefully uncover new ones. The defect collection meeting is considered critical. There is convincing evidence, however, that defect detection in software artifacts is primarily an individual effort and happens during individual preparation and reading (Johnson & Tjahjono, 1998; Votta, 1993), and the purpose of the meeting is mostly to agree on true defects and dismiss false positives. In the state-of-industry practice, the meeting is either removed or not the emphasis anymore. Instead, how the inspectors examine the software artifacts becomes important. To improve an individual's effectiveness, various reading techniques have been proposed and tested. Reading is a key technical activity for verifying and validating software (Basili, 1997). This book is devoted to software reading techniques.

1.2.1   Organization of This Book

Many reading techniques have been developed and tested. This book categorizes them based on their characteristics. Some reading techniques are generic and can be used for many, if not all, software artifacts, while other techniques are only applicable to specific artifacts. This book discusses general reading techniques first, then specific techniques for software artifacts such as requirements, design, and code. The following lists the contents of each chapter.

Chapter 2 discusses the software review procedure. In particular, we discuss Fagan inspection and its extensions. Active design review is discussed in detail as well, since it is the basis of some recent reading techniques such as scenario-based reading.

Chapter 3 defines the terms of software reading and software reading techniques. It discusses reading purposes and classifies existing reading techniques. Ad hoc reading and checklist-based reading are discussed in detail, including various extensions to checklist-based reading, since they are frequently used as baselines and other reading techniques are compared to them. Chapter 3 also discusses differential reading, which can be used to inspect artifacts under evolution.

Chapter 4 focuses on scenario-based reading. Although many reading techniques are classified as scenario-based reading, we discuss defect-based reading, perspective-based reading, and function-point-based reading, as examples of scenario-based reading techniques. Perspective-based reading has been adapted to inspect requirements specifications, design documents, source code files, and user interface usability. The cognitive process of perspective-based reading is also discussed. A simple analytical model is used to shed light on when perspective-based reading could outperform other reading techniques.

Chapter 5 discusses reading techniques specific to requirements specifications. We present a combined reading technique which takes advantages of the strengths of individual reading techniques, while compensating for their weaknesses. Test-driven reading is introduced as an economic reading technique for organizations with limited resources.

Chapter 6 discusses specific reading techniques for design. While most reading techniques gear to find as many defects as possible, not all defects have the same impact on end users. Usage-based reading uses prioritized use-cases as a guiding light to focus readers' attention on defects that matter to users most. This chapter also discusses traceability-based reading that checks for consistency among all design artifacts and between design and requirement artifacts. It is a family of techniques organized as horizontal and vertical readings. Traceability-based reading is also applied to architecture review. Although most of the time we read software artifacts to detect defects, we read software for construction under some circumstances. Scope-based reading is designed to enhance a reader's ability to understand object-oriented application frameworks, which the reader can then use to design and implement their own applications.

Chapter 7 is devoted to specific code reading techniques. It covers reading by stepwise abstraction first and then illustrates how it is extended as abstraction-driven reading for object-oriented code. There are unique challenges in object-oriented code reading. While abstraction-driven reading focuses on the static behavior of an object-oriented system, use-case-driven reading is concerned with the dynamic behavior. Legacy software applications are abundant without much documentation. Task-directed reading can be used to improve code quality and complete the necessary documentation on code and design.

Chapter 8 concludes the book and encourages readers to apply reading techniques to their practice.

1.2.2 Intended Audience and How to Use This Book

This book is intended for software engineering practitioners. We suggest that readers start with Chapters 2 and 3 to get an overview of software inspection and preliminary reading techniques.

- If you are interested in inspecting software requirements specifications, you can continue with Chapters 4 and 5. You may skip non-requirements applications of perspective-based reading in Chapter 4, however.

- If you are interested in inspecting design documents, you can read part of Chapter 4 (Section 4.3.3) and Chapter 6.

- If you are interested in inspecting source code, you can read part of Chapter 4 (Section 4.3.4) and Chapter 7.

- If you are interested in usability inspection, you can read Chapter 4 (Section 4.3.5).

This book is also intended for software engineering students and can be used to supplement courses such as software engineering, software quality, and software testing. As students are preparing themselves to join the software industry as software engineers, it is beneficial for students to read the entire book.

This book can be used by software engineering researchers, particularly if you are interested in software quality assurance, software inspection, and software reading. This book has the most comprehensive material on software reading. You can find references to the original articles where particular reading techniques were first proposed, as well as information on the most recent developments and experiences with those reading techniques.

1.3 References

(Basili, 1987) V.R. Basili and R.W. Selby, Comparing the effectiveness of software testing strategies, IEEE Transactions on Software Engineering, vol.13, no,12m pp.1278-1296, 1987.

(Basili, 1997) V.R. Basili, Evolving and packaging reading technologies, Journal of Systems and Software, vol.38, no.1, pp.3-12, 1997.

(Briand, 1998) L. Briand, K. EI Emam, O. Laitenberger, and T. Fussbroich, Using simulation to build inspection efficiency benchmarks for development projects, Proceedings of the International Conference on Software Engineering, pp.340-349, 1998.

(Doolan, 1992) E. Doolan, Experience with Fagan's inspection method, Software Practice and Experience, vol.22, o.2, pp.173-182, 1992.

(Fagan, 1976) M.E. Fagan, Design and code inspections to reduce errors in program development, IBM Systems Journal, vol.15, no.3, pp.182-211, 1976.

(Gilb, 1993) T. Gilb and D. Graham, Software Inspection, Addison-Wesley, 1993.

(IEEE 1028) IEEE Std 1028-2008, IEEE Standard for Software Reviews and Audits, 2008.

(Johnson, 1998) P.M. Johnson and D. Tjahjono, Does every inspection really need a meeting? Empirical Software Engineering, vol.3, pp.9-35, 1998.

(Juristo, 2003) N. Juristo and S. Vegas, Functional testing, structural testing and code reading: what fault type do they each detect? Lecture Notes in Computer Science, vol.2765, pp.208-232, 2003.

(Laitenberger, 2002) O. Laitenberger, A survey of software inspection technologies, in Handbook on Software Engineering ad Knowledge Engineering, vol.2, pp.517-555, 2002.

(Mantyla, 2009) M.V. Mantyla and C. Lassenius, What types of defects are really discovered in code reviews? IEEE Transactions on Software Engineering, vol.35, no.3, pp.430-448, 2009.

(McConnell, 2004) S. McConnell, Code Complete, 2nd ed., Microsoft Press, 2004.

(Porter, 1996) A. Porter, H. Siy, and L. Votta, A review of software inspections, Advances in Computers, vol.42, pp.39-76, 1996.

(Russell, 1991) G.W. Russell, Experience with inspection in ultra large-scale developments, IEEE Software, vol.8, no.1, pp.25-31, 1991.

(Votta, 1993) L.G. Votta Jr., Does every inspection need a meeting? Proceedings of the ACM SIGSOFT Symposium on Foundations of Software Engineering, pp.107-114, 1993.

CHAPTER 2

Software Review Procedures

Although software peer review has been practiced for more than four decades, software literature uses inconsistent and in many cases conflicting terms to refer to more or less the same activities. According to IEEE Std-1028 (IEEE 1028), inspection is "A visual examination of a software product to detect and identify software anomalies, including errors and deviations from standards and specifications," and review is "A process or meeting during which a software product, set of software product, or a software process is presented to project personnel, managers, users, customers, user representatives, auditors or other interested parties for examination, comment or approval." The standard defines five types of reviews (management reviews, technical reviews, inspections, walkthroughs, and audits), and software inspections are a kind of review. We use review as a general term. This chapter describes a generic procedure for software review, then treats Fagan inspection and active design review in more detail. Factors impacting the effectiveness of software review are also discussed.

2.1 A Generic Software Review Procedure

All software review procedures share some commonalities. IEEE Std-1028 listed the following five steps for all the five types of reviews: (1) planning the review, (2) overview of the procedures, (3) preparation, (4) examination/evaluation/recording of results, and (5) rework/follow-up (IEEE 1028). Laitenberger used a reference model for software inspection processes, which has six phases: planning, overview, defect detection, defect collection, defect correction, and follow-up (Laitenberger, 2002). Tian abstracted a generic software review procedure with three steps, and various software review procedures can be considered as extensions to or specialization of this generic one (Tian, 2005). We discuss Tian's abstraction in this section.

The generic software review procedure has three stages of activities: planning and preparation, conducting the review, and corrections and follow-up, as illustrated in Figure 2-1.

Figure 2-1. *A generic software review procedure*

Y.-M. Zhu, *Software Reading Techniques*, DOI 10.1007/978-1-4842-2346-8_2

In the planning and preparation stage, one typically defines objectives of a review and decides what artifacts are subject to review, who will create them, who will review them and who else will be involved and in what capacity, when will the review happen, and what are the overall process and follow-up activities if needed. Before conducting a review, the document authors will assemble the material, decide the avenue for the review, and handle the review logistics, etc.

In the reviewing stage, people get together as a team face-to-face or on-line, synchronously or asynchronously. The team goes through the material under review in some pre-determined manner, discusses issues reported before the meeting or spotted in session, agrees on the observation or dismisses false positives. The focus of this stage is to uncover and collate issues in the document under review, and hence it is often called collection. In the end, the review team agrees whether a follow-up review session is warranted.

In the correction and follow-up stage, the author corrects issues that have surfaced during the review. The dispositions of the issues shall be agreed by the review team and the corrections or fixes shall be verified. A follow-up review can be conducted for that purpose, if the extent of changes is large; otherwise a lightweight follow-up shall suffice.

We discuss two classical software review procedures, namely Fagan inspection and active design review, which can be considered as an extension to this generic review. We use the term Fagan inspection for historical reasons.

Software review or inspection is independent of software development models, like waterfall or agile. Software review can be applied to a software artifact as soon as it is ready for review. Software review is considered a best practice and it is an important activity of software quality assurance (Tian, 2005).

2.2   Fagan Inspection and Extensions

The earliest and most influential software review procedure was proposed by Fagan in 1976 (Fagan, 1976). The method was initially intended for design and code inspection and later adapted to inspect virtually any software artifacts such as requirements, user documentation, and test plans and test cases as long as such artifacts can be made visible and readable (Fagan, 1986). Fagan inspection has been so influential that it is almost synonymous with the term inspection.

2.2.1   Fagan Inspection

Fagan inspection consists of six steps or operations as originally called: planning, overview, preparation, inspection, rework, and follow-up, as depicted in Figure 2-2. The planning step was not in Fagan's seminal paper (Fagan, 1976) but was added later (Fagan, 1986).

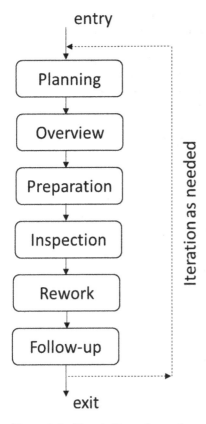

Figure 2-2. *Steps in Fagan inspection*

We discuss these six steps in the context of design and code inspection. The principal ideas behind Fagan inspection can be applied to inspecting any software artifacts.

- Planning: The objectives of the planning step are to define inspection entry criteria for the materials subject to inspect, to arrange the availability of the appropriate participants, and to arrange the meeting place and time.

- Overview: The objectives of the overview step are communication and education, as well as assigning the inspection roles to participants. This step involves the whole inspection team. Typically a meeting is held, during which the project overview and the specifics of the artifact to be inspected are given. The inspection materials are distributed at the end of the meeting.

- Preparation: The objective of the preparation step is for participants to study the material individually to fulfill their respective roles. One of the key ideas in the inspection is to assign different roles to the individual participants based on their respective expertise. The roles of the participants are discussed below. To facilitate the preparation, a checklist of recent error types can be used, or other kinds of reading techniques can be adopted. Software reading techniques are discussed in the rest of the book.

- Inspection: The objective of the inspection step is to find the errors in the material under inspection. A formal meeting is held and the entire team participates in the discussion. At the beginning of the meeting, if code files are under inspection, then the implementer (author) can show the implementation of the design. In the course of the meeting, errors are discussed; false positives are dismissed and true errors are recognized and noted, with possible error type classification and severity identification. It is important to note that the team should not hunt for solution nor discuss alternatives. After the inspection has been held, a written report of the findings is released in a timely manner.

- Rework: The objective of the rework step is to fix all errors or provide other responses. The author of the software artifact is responsible for the rework and responses.

- Follow-up: The objective of the follow-up step is to ensure all fixes are effective and there are no newly introduced problems. The moderator decides if another round of inspection is needed. For example, if the errors are minor and the changes are limited, then he can declare there is no need for another round of inspection. Regardless of whether there is another round of inspection, the team needs to pay attention to "bad fixes." Empirical data show that almost one of every six fixes are incorrect or create other defects (Fagan, 1986).

We can view Fagan inspection in the framework of the generic review. The first three steps of the Fagan inspection—planning, overview, and preparation—fit into the "planning and preparation" step in the generic review diagram; the inspection step of the Fagan inspection directly maps to the "review" block in the generic review; and the last two steps of the Fagan inspection—rework and follow-up—map to the "correction and follow-up" step in the generic review. Both the generic review and the Fagan inspection allow an optional iteration.

As mentioned above, the Fagan inspection defines the participant roles that each participant plays. There are four roles: moderator, author, reader, and tester. The moderator leads the inspection team and takes care of logistics; the other roles represent the viewpoints of those with their respective expertise during the inspection.

The moderator is the key person in a successful inspection. He or she possesses strong interpersonal and leadership skills, coaches and guides the inspection team, and handles meeting logistics, including scheduling the meeting and publishing the outcome of the inspection. The moderator must be neutral and objective. The author is the person who created the software artifacts under inspection. The author is responsible for producing the artifacts and fixing the errors in the artifacts, with possible help from others. The reader is an experienced peer who can be a subject matter expert on the software artifact under inspection. The tester is responsible for writing and/or executing test cases for the software module or the product.

The Fagan inspection team typically consists of four people, large enough to allow group interaction to detect errors in software artifacts but small enough to allow individual voices to be heard. To have a healthy group dynamic, an ideal mix of participants can include people with different background and experience.

The Fagan-style reviews have a few noticeable drawbacks. One of them is the heavy process involved, which requires a series of formal meetings and documentations. This limitation is overcome by the introduction of modern lightweight reviews. The other drawback is that the quality of review varies widely, since the participants may be passively engaged with the review. This latter shortcoming is remediated by the active review, which is discussed in the next subsection.

2.2.2 Extensions to Fagan Inspection

It has been 40 years since Fagan published the Fagan inspection. Fagan inspection has been studied by researchers and embraced by practitioners (Aurum et al., 2002; Kollanus & Koskinen, 2009). The inspection procedure has been extended in different ways to further improve its efficiency or customize to unique situations. We summarize a few important extensions below.

2.2.2.1 Meeting or No Meeting

Proposed improvements to Fagan inspection often center on the importance and cost of group meetings, particularly the defect collection meeting. Fagan insisted on having a defect collection meeting, but other researchers questioned the importance of meetings. Reasons often cited to support a team meeting include:

- Synergy: More people working together will find more defects than they would working alone.

- Learning and knowledge sharing: Meetings are good opportunity for beginners to gain domain knowledge from experienced participants.

- Milestone: Meetings serve as project milestones.

However, it takes time and effect to schedule a group meeting, particularly when it involves many people. Researchers questioned whether the meeting creates synergy at all. Votta (1993) reported that most defects were found during the individual preparation stage, which was confirmed by many others, including Porter et al. (1995). Johnson and Tjahjono (1998) also reported that meeting-based reviews were significantly more costly than non-meeting-based reviews, and meeting-based reviews did not detect significantly more detects. However, meeting-based reviews were significantly better at reducing false positive defects, and reviewers preferred meeting-based reviews over non-meeting-based reviews.

The general consensus now is to not have a large group meeting or at least not emphasize it. A few alternatives are proposed to replace full-team meetings. As an example, a few experts can go through defects reported by individual reviewers during their preparation and decide the nature of defects (true vs false positives) (Sauer et al., 2000). Meeting-less inspections further evolved into modern lightweight inspections, which are discussed later.

2.2.2.2   What Is the Right Team Size?

Fagan suggested a team size of 4 people. A large team presumably allows a different kind of defects to be found since each reviewer has different expertise and experience. The argument of cost-effectiveness favors a smaller team. Bisant and Lyle (1989) proposed a two-person inspection involving just the author and reviewer, which makes the inspection accessible to teams or organizations that don't have access to larger team resources. Porter and colleagues (1997) conducted code inspection experiments in situ by varying the number of inspectors on each inspection team (1, 2, or 4) and concluded that, while 1 inspector was significantly less effective than 2 or 4 inspectors, there was little difference in the inspection effectiveness of 2 or 4 inspectors.

Instead of a single large team, Schneider et al. (1992) split a large team into N smaller teams for critical projects, let the N smaller teams to inspect requirements documents on parallel and independently, and aggregated defects from each smaller team at the end, which is known as N-fold inspection. They reported that independent teams found more defects than a single team.

Perhaps there is no optimal team size. The right team size will depend on the artifacts under review (types and complexity), organizational environment (whether it has access to large resources), etc. For important documents such as a requirements specification, more points of view are certainly beneficial. It is also a good idea to have more people to review the design than code. Complex artifacts also warrant more independent reviewers with different expertise.

2.2.2.3   Other Extensions

Gilb and Graham (1993) introduced a process brainstorming meeting right after the inspection meeting. This meeting's function is root cause analysis so that similar defects can be prevented from happening in future projects or activities in the same project.

Knight and Myers (1993) studied a phased inspection (for code inspections), which consists of multiple phases or mini-inspections, each focusing on detecting one class of defects such as issues with language, code layout, programming constructs, etc. Defects have to be fixed before the next phase can start.

Many software artifacts are generated in the course of project development. It might be infeasible to inspect all documents due to resource constraints. To address this concern, Thelin et al. (2004) developed a sampling-driven inspection, which utilizes a pre-inspection to identify a partial list of documents that can benefit from a focused inspection. The decision can also be based on the historical defect data and the characteristics of the document itself, e.g., code complexity metrics.

2.3   Active Design Review and Extensions

The active design review was introduced by Parnas and Weiss (1985). Although the publication came much later than Fagan's, according to Weiss, they conceived the idea independently about the same time as Fagan published his work.

2.3.1   Active Design Review

The purpose of design review is to find errors in design and its documentation. There are many kinds of design errors—e.g., inconsistency (different assumptions), inefficiency (inefficient to implement or use), ambiguity (allows different interpretation or lack of clarity), and inflexibility (does not accommodate change). Conventional reviews such as Fagan inspection tend to be incomplete and shallow. Parnas and Weiss noticed that reviews have variable quality and many factors contributed to it:

- The amount, quality, and time of delivery of the design documentation varied widely

- The time that the reviewers put in preparation varied widely

- The participation of the reviewers varied widely

- The expertise and roles of the reviewers varied widely

The active design review was proposed to reduce the variability and promote a consistent review quality. The key part of the active design review is the use of questionnaires to define the reviewer's responsibilities and to ensure they play a more active role. The main ideas behind the active design review, when compared to the Fagan-style review, include:

- The required knowledge and skills reviewers possess are explicitly identified before selecting the reviewers.

- Reviewers focus their efforts on the design aspects related to their experience and expertise.

- The designers pose questions to the reviewers rather than the reviewers asking questions. Each question is carefully designed such that its answer requires careful study of the design under review or some aspects of the design.

- Reviewers are actively involved in the review and make positive assertions on the design instead of merely skimming over the design for obvious or trivial errors.

- Reviewers and designers meet in a small group to resolves issues.

An active design review has five phases:

1. Make the design reviewable. A good design shall be well structured, simple, efficient, adequate, flexible, practical, implementable, and standardized. Design assumptions shall be made explicit. The design document can include redundant information for error and consistency checking. The document shall be structured in such a way that modules and submodules can be reviewed separately.

2. Identify the review types. A design review shall be focused and have a well-defined purpose. It is thus easy to identify expertise needed to support the review. Different reviews can concentrate on detecting different error types such as assumption validity, sufficiency, consistency between assumptions and functions, and adequacy.

3. Classify reviewers. Reviewers shall be specialists, potential users, those familiar with the design methods and technologies used, or those skilled at finding issues. The review shall exploit the skills and knowledge of the reviewers to detect as many errors as possible.

4. Design questionnaires. The questions shall not be trivial. They ensure the reviewers take an active role and use the design document to answer the questions. The questions shall be rephrased to avoid yes/no answers.

5. Conduct the review. There is no big meeting. Instead, the designer and reviewer have 1:1 or small group discussion. This phase has three stages:

    a. An overview meeting to discuss the material under review and how the process works.

    b. Assign reviewers to specific sections of the document, with a deadline of when the questions shall be answered and returned to the designer. The designer/reviewer meeting is also scheduled.

    c. The designer collects and reads the completed questionnaires and meets with reviewers individually to understand and resolve questions. The designer also updates the design document afterwards.

The active design review has a few challenges. It is usually hard to find subject matter experts to serve as reviewers and get their time commitment, as everyone has a busy schedule and other commitments in the same or different projects. There is no big meeting, and review is managed as individual tasks, thus it takes diligence to keep the review on track and complete on time. Lastly, it takes significant effort to design a set of questions whose answers are not obvious and easy to find. The questions for the reviewers to answer shall be carefully designed and non-trivial, which forces reviewers to play the roles of users of the design and write a program to implement the design. Answering the questions makes the reviewer active. The questions shall also be tailored to the reviewer's expertise and the aspects of the document under review.

2.3.2   Extensions to the Active Design Review

Britcher (1988) took the active design review one step further by incorporating correctness arguments into inspection. The artifact author and inspectors collaborate in the pursuit of correctness, developing questions and answers together centering on four program attributes: topology, algebra, invariance, and robustness. The purpose for this extension is not to improve inspections but to improve programming.

The active design review was espoused the architecture tradeoff analysis method and the new method is called active review for intermediate designs (Clements, 2000). The hybrid method fills a niche that only a portion of a system, not a complete architecture, is available, but the designer would like to get early feedback on the design approach.

The ideas behind the active design review have been used in scenario-based reading, as we will discuss in Chapter 4.

2.4   Other Types of Reviews

In addition to the Fagan Inspection and active design review and their extensions, many different kinds of software review exist in practice with different levels of discipline and flexibility. There are, however, no commonly agreed-upon definitions of terms. The usages are generally inconsistent, which causes confusions in many cases. Even for the same type of reviews, the levels of procedural details can vary significantly. Fagan, in his seminal paper, recognized that walkthroughs were practiced in many different places with varying regularity and thoroughness (Fagan, 1976). It was also reported that one person's walkthrough can be another person's inspection (Wiegers, 2001).

Wiegers (2001) organized different types of reviews based on their levels of formality and rigor. He discussed, in the decreasing order of formality, inspection, team review, walkthrough, pair programming, peer desk-check or pass-around, and ad hoc review. Cohen et al. (2006) discussed five types of review: formal inspections, over-the-shoulder reviews (screen or desk reviews), e-mail pass-around reviews, pair programming, and tool-assisted reviews. IEEE Standard for Software Reviews and Audits defined five types of software reviews (management reviews, technical reviews, inspections, walkthroughs, and software audits) (IEEE 1028). In terms of formality, walkthroughs are least formal, inspections less formal, followed by management and technical reviews, with audits being most formal. These types of reviews and audits are considered systematic, with the following attributes: team participation, documented results of the review, and documented procedures for conducting the review.

The review or inspection procedures mentioned above are applicable to any software artifacts, with the exception of pair programming, which is mostly applicable to source code. There are specific review procedures for particular kinds of software artifacts as well. Given the importance of software architecture in software life cycle, architecture review and evaluation methods were an active area of research and now have become mature. We use techniques (or procedures) and methods as synonyms, although some authors distinguish them deliberately (Basili, 1997). The ways to assess software architectures are packaged as "methods" in literature. Interested readers can find more information in books on architecture evaluation such as Clements et al. (2002).

We do not intend to define various types of reviews, rather suggest adopting the definitions in the IEEE standard. We do want to point out the trend in industry practices. A lightweight process is strongly favored by practitioners due to their busy schedule and heavy workload, and therefore the synchronous, real-time, face-to-face meeting in Fagan inspection can be impractical. The synergy of the defect collection meeting has been questioned and the community generally agrees that its value is marginal. Thus software reviews can be conducted without meetings. The IEEE standard permits reviews to be held without physical meeting in a single location. Given the advancement of telecommunication and telepresence, physical meetings can be replaced with telephone conference, video conference, web conference, or other groupware and group electronic communications.

Software tools to support software reviews also have made progress. Web-based tools allow authors to upload software artifacts to web servers, invite reviewers, and set up a review online. Reviewers can enter review comments online and see each other's comments instantly. Issues raised during review are tracked by tools for closure. Synchronous and asynchronous notifications keep the author and reviewers in the same loop on progress. Review metrics are automatically collected to provide input for future process improvement. With these features and capabilities, the overhead of classic inspections is alleviated.

At least for code review, many organizations, including Facebook, Google, and Microsoft, are adopting lightweight, tool-assisted reviews (Bacchelli & Bird, 2013). Bacchelli and Bird called this modern code review. Referring to Fagan's inspection, only preparation, collection (inspection), and rework stages are present in the lightweight review, and defect collection is facilitated with tools. There is empirical evidence that support the efficiency and effectiveness of the lightweight, tool-assisted modern practice (Bacchelli & Bird, 2013; Cohen et al., 2006).

2.5   Factors Impacting Software Reviews

When the purpose of software reviews is to detect defects in the software artifacts, one is interested in how many defects are detected and how quickly they are detected. The number of detected defects is related to the effectiveness of software reviews. The more defects are detected, the more effective a software review is. How quickly defects are detected (number of detected defects per unit of time) is related to the efficiency and cost of software reviews. The quicker the defects are detected, the lower the cost of software review. Many factors impact the effectiveness and efficiency of software reviews, and individual performance, meetings, preparation, the amount of inspected materials, team size, tools, and training are frequently mentioned factors. Meetings and team sizes have been discussed earlier. Both commercial and research tools exist to support software inspection, mostly in the areas of asynchronous communication, artifact comprehension and visualization, and defect tracking. We discuss the remaining factors here.

> **Individual performance**. Large difference (more than 10 times) in individual performance in software engineering was observed a long time ago (Boehm, 1981). Hatton (2008) recently reported the same in code inspection. A few attributes contributed to the difference, including expertise on the programming language (Knight, 1993) and software reading expertise (Sauer, 2000). The rest of the book is devoted to software reading techniques.

Preparation. The importance of individual preparation to defect detection was reported by many authors—e.g., Gilb (1993). The more time a reviewer spent on preparation, the more defects are typically reported. It is generally agreed that most defects are found during individual's preparation phase before defects are aggregated.

Amount of materials. Due to people's limited attention span, when the amount of materials to be inspected is large, readers become overwhelmed and fatigued, which negatively impacts the review effectiveness. For code inspection, the rate of inspection often suggested in literature is 100-200 lines of code per hour. If readers are not given enough time to examine the material, then the inspection loses its rigor and readers tend to report trivial findings.

Training. The level of training readers receive impacts the review effectiveness. This should not be a surprise, given the importance of individual's skills in inspection. Researchers found that practical training on defect finding skills was more impactful than the training on process.

Software development is a highly personal endeavor. Without care, software review or inspection can easily cause anxiety and tension among participants. The social psychological effects of computer programming were recognized from the early days of programming (Weinberg, 1998). Weinberg published his famous book, The Psychology of Computer Programming, in 1971, before Fagan inspection was introduced and practiced. Authors should have a thick skin and have their egos checked when participating in the reviews. Reviewers should recognize the IKEA effect on the artifact authors. The IKEA effect is a cognitive bias in which the artifact creators place a disproportionately higher value on the artifact they created (Norton et al., 2012). More labors lead to deeper affection. Successful inspection depends on the individual capability of each team member and how well individuals work in teams.

Before we close this section, let's discuss the eight maxims Kelly and Shepard (2004) compiled based on their observations, which focus on people forces at work in inspections.

1. Use structured inspection techniques. By inspection techniques, Kelly and Shepard meant reading techniques. The techniques shall be appropriate for the inspection goals and inspectors' experience.

2. Set standards of acceptability. Inspections are expensive. There should be entrance criteria to start the inspection. Artifacts shall be cleaned up and superficial issues shall be rooted out, preferably with tools, before inspections start.

3. Match skills to tasks. If skills and tasks are matched, both effectiveness and the comfort level of the inspector improve. Inspectors who are familiar with the artifacts under review shall be chosen first. Skills here also include soft skills such as verbal and written communication skills, which are needed to interact with artifact authors.

4. Find physical, mental, and schedule space. Inspections are mentally demanding and require concentration for an extended period of time. Inspection shall be conducted at a quiet place without interruption, and inspectors shall be given enough time to complete the inspection.

5. Encourage an inspection-based process. At minimum, the inspection shall be planned, and the project schedule shall reflect that. Roles and responsibilities shall be clearly specified ahead of time.

6. Promote responsibility, ownership, and authority. Responsibility and ownership lead to improved inspection efforts. Inspectors and authors jointly own the artifact and are responsible to its quality. Inspectors shall be granted the authority to access needed documents and resources to complete the inspection.

7. Ensure clear inspection goals are set. Clear goals affect the scope of the inspection. It shall be clear to all participants if alternative solutions shall be proposed or not. Also ensure terminologies are defined and used consistently to avoid potential confusion.

8. Use metrics cautiously. Metrics can be used and interpreted in different ways. There is no commonly agreed-upon definition of "defect," nor its granularity and severity. The number of defects is strongly related to the complexity of the task itself. Metrics shall not be used to evaluate an individual's job performance.

2.6 Summary

Software review and inspection is considered a best practice and has been practiced over four decades. There are many flavors of reviews and inspections. We focused on the classic Fagan inspection and active design review, as well as their various extensions. Fagan inspection is not only the first formal inspection method but also the foundation of many other modified versions. The ideas of the active design review are used in many software reading techniques, as we shall see in later chapters.

Laitenberger and DeBaud (2000) contextualized software inspection in the software lifecycle. They provided suggestions on how Fagan inspection and its various extensions can be customized to inspect different software artifacts created during the software lifecycle, with different reading techniques. IEEE Std 1028 has a comprehensive list of software artifacts that can be subject to review or inspection (IEEE 1028). Many factors impact the performance of software reviews and inspections, chief among which is individual factor. It is well established that software review and inspection is primarily an individual, not a group, activity. How the reviewer reads and extracts information from the software artifact under review impacts his or her performance. The rest of the book focuses on reading techniques, which are meant to equip the readers and enhance their review and inspection capacities.

2.7 References

(Aurum, 2002) A. Aurum, H. Petersson, and C. Wohlin, State-of-the-art: software inspections after 25 years, Software Testing, Verification and Reliability, vol.12, pp.133-154, 2002.

(Bacchelli, 2013) A. Bacchelli and C. Bird, Expectations, outcomes, and challenges of modern code review, Proceedings of the 35th IEEE/ACM International Conference on Software Engineering, pp.712-721, 2013.

(Basili, 1997) V.R. Basili, Evolving and packaging reading technologies, Journal of Systems and Software, vol.38, no.1, pp.3-12, 1997.

(Bisant, 1989) D.B. Bisant and J.R. Lyle, A two-person inspection method to improve programming productivity, IEEE Transactions on Software Engineering, vol.15, no.10, pp.1294-1304, 1989.

(Boehm, 1981) B.W. Boehm, Software Engineering Economics, Prentice-Hall, 1981.

(Britcher, 1988) R.N. Britcher, Using inspections to investigate program correctness, IEEE Computer, vol.21, no.11, pp.38-44, 1988.

(Clements, 2000) P.C. Clements, Active Reviews for Intermediate Designs, Technical Note, CMU/SEI-2000-TN-009, 2000.

(Clements, 2002) P. Clements, R. Kazman, and M. Klein, Evaluating Software Architectures: Methods and Case Studies, Addison-Wesley, 2002.

(Cohen, 2006) J. Cohen, S. Teleki, and E. Brown, Best Kept Secrets of Peer Code Review, Smart Bear Inc., 2006.

(Fagan, 1976) M.E. Fagan, Design and code inspections to reduce errors in program development, IBM Systems Journal, vol.15, no.3, pp.182-211, 1976.

(Fagan, 1986) M.E. Fagan, Advances in software inspections, IEEE Transactions on Software Engineering, vol.12, no.7, pp.744-751, July 1986.

(Gilb, 1993) T. Gilb and D. Graham, Software Inspection, Addison-Wesley, 1993.

(Hatton, 2008) L. Hatton, Testing the value of checklists in code inspections, IEEE Software, vol.25, no.4, pp.82-88, 2008.

(IEEE 1028) IEEE Std 1028-2008, IEEE Standard for Software Reviews and Audits, 2008.

(Johnson, 1998) P.M. Johnson and D. Tjahjono, Does every inspection really need a meeting? Empirical Software Engineering, vol.3, pp.9-35, 1998.

(Kelly, 2004) D. Kelly and T. Shepard, Eight maxims for software inspectors, Software Testing, Verification and Reliability, vol.14, pp.243-256, 2004.

(Knight, 1993) J.C. Knight and E.A. Myers, An improved inspection technique, Communications of the ACM, vol.36, no.11, pp.51-61, 1993.

(Kollanus, 2009) S. Kollanus and J. Koskinen, Survey of software inspection research, The Open Software Engineering Journal, vol.3, pp.15-34, 2009.

(Laitenberger, 2000) O. Laitenberger and J.M. DeBaud, An encompassing life cycle centric survey of software inspection, Journal of Systems and Software, vol.50, no.1, pp.5-31, 2000.

(Laitenberger, 2002) O. Laitenberger, A survey of software inspection technologies, in Handbook on Software Engineering and Knowledge Engineering, vol.2 Emerging Technologies, World Scientific, 2002.

(Norton, 2012) M.I. Norton, D. Mochon, and D. Ariely, The IKEA effect: When labor leads to love, Journal of Consumer Psychology, vol.22, no.3, pp.453-460, 2012.

(Parnas, 1985) D.L. Parnas and D.M. Weiss, Active design reviews: principles and practices, 8th International conference on Software Engineering, pp.215-222, 1985.

(Porter, 1995) A.A. Porter, L.G. Votta, and V.R. Basili, Comparing detection methods for software requirements inspection: A replicated experiment, IEEE Transactions on Software Engineering, vol.21, no.6, pp.563-575, 1995.

(Porter, 1997) A.A. Porter, H.P. Siy, C.A. Toman, and L.G. Votta, An experiment to assess the cost-benefit of code inspections in large scale software development, IEEE Transactions on Software Engineering, vol.23, no.6, pp.329-346, 1997.

(Sauer, 2000) C. Sauer, D.R. Jeffery, L. Land, and P. Yetton, The effectiveness of software development technical reviews: A behaviorally motivated program of research, IEEE Transactions on Software Engineering, vol.26, no.1, pp.1-14, 2000.

(Schneider, 1992) M. Schneider, J. Martin, and W. Tsai, An experimental study of fault detection in user requirements documents, ACM Transactions on Software Engineering and Methodology, vol.1, no.2, pp.188-204, 1992.

(Thelin, 2004) T. Thelin, H. Petersson, P. Runeson, and C. Wohlin, Applying sampling to improve software inspections, Journal of Systems and Software, vol.73, no.2, pp.257-269, 2004.

(Tian, 2005) J. Tian, Software Quality Engineering: testing, quality assurance, and quantifiable improvement, IEEE Computer Society Press, 2005.

(Votta, 1993) L.G. Votta Jr., Does every inspection need a meeting? Proceedings of the ACM SIGSOFT Symposium on Foundations of Software Engineering, pp.107-114, 1993.

(Weinberg, 1998) G.M. Weinberg, The Psychology of Computer Programming: Silver Anniversary Edition, Dorset House, 1998.

(Wiegers, 2001) K.E. Wiegers, Peer Reviews in Software: A Practical Guide, Addison-Wesley Professional, 2001.

CHAPTER 3

■ ■ ■

Basic Software Reading Techniques

As software professionals we were all trained to create software artifacts. For example, requirements engineers were taught how to define, document, and maintain requirements; software designers were trained to conceptualize the system, come up with architecture to deliver ever-demanding user experience, and document the architectural design; software developers were trained to write programs in programming languages using various constructs and concepts. However, we were not taught how to read those artifacts and source code authored by others.

There is ample empirical evidence that the software review is primarily an individual effort and many anomalies are uncovered in the course of individual reading (Johnson & Tjahjono, 1998; Votta, 1993). Thus the kinds of reading techniques the individual uses are paramount to the outcome and effectiveness of software review. This chapter defines what software reading is and surveys the basic software reading techniques.

3.1   Introduction to Software Reading

Everyone who received primary education knows how to read. However, the effectiveness of reading varies. Wikipedia defines reading as (https://en.wikipedia.org/wiki/Reading_(process), accessed on Dec. 15, 2015. http://www.encyclopedia.com/topic/reading.aspx essentially contains the same elements as Wikipedia summarizes)

> *Reading is a complex cognitive process of decoding symbols in order to construct or derive meaning. ... [I]t is a complex interaction between the text and the reader which is shaped by the reader's prior knowledge, experiences, attitude, ... The reading process requires continuous practice, development, and refinement. In addition, reading requires creativity and critical analysis. ... Readers integrate the words they have read into their existing framework of knowledge and schema.*

Based on this discussion, we conclude that (1) reading has a purpose, (2) the reader's background plays a role in reading, (3) reading techniques can be learned, and (4) reading requires critical analysis. Those general characteristics exhibit in software reading as well.

© Yang-Ming Zhu 2016
Y.-M. Zhu, *Software Reading Techniques*, DOI 10.1007/978-1-4842-2346-8_3

3.1.1   Definition of Software Reading

Based on the Encyclopedia of Software Engineering (Shull, 2002), software reading is defined as the process by which a developer gains an understanding of the information encoded in a work product sufficient to accomplish a particular task. We adopt the same definition. The "work product" refers to the software artifact, ranging from requirements specification, design documentation, code files, test plan, test cases, test reports, to user documentation, etc. The "particular task" is related to the purpose of reading, whether the reading is for gaining knowledge of the system, detecting defects, or implementing the design. The purposes of reading are systematically treated in the next subsection.

Associated with software reading is the software reading technique. Again, based on the Encyclopedia of Software Engineering (Shull, 2002), a software reading technique is a series of steps for the individual analysis of a textual software product to achieve the understanding needed for a particular task. A series of steps is a set of instructions that guide the reader how to read the artifacts, what areas to focus on, and what problems to look for. Again software reading is primarily an individual activity.

Ever since the Fagan inspection was introduced, it was recognized that some sort of reading technique was needed. Fagan suggested using checklists (Fagan, 1976). By now there is a big body of knowledge on software reading techniques. The software reading technique has become an active research area since 1994 after Porter and Votta (1994) published their paper on scenario-based reading. Between 1980 and 2008, 16% of software inspection research papers were on software reading techniques (Kollanus & Koskinen, 2009). This chapter surveys a few early and popular reading techniques. Latter chapters discuss more advanced or specialized reading techniques.

3.1.2   Purposes of Software Reading

We read software artifacts to accomplish a particular task. The task is defined by the purpose of reading. Broadly speaking, we read software for analysis and for construction (Basili et al., 1996).

In reading for analysis, we read and understand the document, then analyze and assess the qualities and characteristics of the document. The primary objective of reading for analysis is to detect defects in the document. When reading the requirements specifications, we may detect various types of requirement errors such as incorrect facts, omission, ambiguity, and inconsistency. When reading the code, we may detect various types of coding errors such as logic errors, assumption errors, incorrect function calls, etc. Other objectives of reading for analysis include performance predictions, requirement tracing, usability assessment, etc. One of the main reasons to have an architecture document is to support analysis and prediction (Clements et al., 2011). For example, we can predict system performance by using queue theory when there are one or multiple processing queues involved. By reading the system requirements specification and subsystem requirements specification, we can reason whether the system requirements specification is sufficiently decomposed to the subsystem requirements specification, and whether the subsystem requirements specification can indeed trace back to its system requirements specification origin and have a sufficient coverage of the system requirements specification.

In reading for construction, we attempt to identify if any requirements, design, code or test cases can be reused in the same project or in a different project. We also examine the high-level design document to come up with the low-level design or read the design document to see how we may implement the design properly. Sometimes we read the software just to gain the knowledge. It might be true, however, we have an interest to maintain the software in future.

Reading for defect detection is the focus of most researchers and is also the main concern of this book.

3.1.3   Taxonomy of Software Reading Techniques

Software reading techniques can be classified along different dimensions. Based on whether the reading technique is structured (systematic) or not, the reading techniques can be put into the following categories:

- Unstructured, or unsystematic reading: Ad hoc reading falls into this category. Ad hoc reading is discussed in this chapter.

- Semi-structured reading: Checklist-based reading is in this group and is also discussed in detail in this chapter.

- Structured or systematic reading: Perspective-based reading falls into this group, along with many other techniques. These reading techniques collect knowledge about the best practices for defect detection into a single procedure. To some extent, they serve a similar role as design patterns to design. These techniques are covered in other chapters of this book.

When we discuss the benefits and shortcomings of each reading technique, keep in mind that structures of any kind simultaneously enable and limit human activities. This is known as the Paradox of Structure (Jablokow, 2003): While a structured reading technique enables one to find anomalies in the software artifact, the same reading technique may limit one to find anomalies only in certain categories.

Reading techniques can be classified according to the software artifacts to which they are applied. For example, checklist-based reading can be applied to review almost every software artifact, while stepwise abstraction, which is discussed in a later chapter, is only applicable to code review.

3.2   Ad hoc Reading

When there is no specific method provided to the reader to detect issues or defects in the software artifacts under review, we call it an ad hoc reading. This is an unstructured, or unsystematic, reading technique. The reader simply attempts to uncover as many issues and defects as possible by examining the artifact using whatever intuition, skills, knowledge, and experience he or she may have. The effectiveness of the ad hoc reading is entirely up to the individual reader. The individual defect detection performance can vary by a factor of 10 in terms of defects found per unit time (Hatton, 2008). Nevertheless, it is the most common reading technique.

One of the advantages of the ad hoc reading is that there is no training needed for the reader. However, it has many disadvantages, among which is the wide variability of the results. In fact, the outcome to a large extent depends on the skills, knowledge, and experience of the reader. It is slow for readers to acquire expertise; thus inexperienced readers will not be productive when reviewing software artifacts to uncover issues. Once the expertise has been acquired, it is very difficult to teach or transfer the expertise to others. Since the effectiveness of the ad hoc reading depends on individual expertise, readers adopting this reading technique may miss major areas of concern.

3.3   Checklist-Based Reading

Checklists are ubiquitous. You may use a shopping list. Grade school kids often have a school supply list for the next school year. If you are planning a family vacation, you most likely have a packing list. The example list goes on and on.

Checklists are widely used in software reading and they serve a similar purpose as the above-mentioned checklists do. In fact, Fagan (1976) suggested using a checklist during software inspection in his seminal paper. Since then checklists for software review have flourished. In the 1999 survey, Brykczynski (1999) reviewed 117 checklists. And checklists are continuously being proposed for software reading.

3.3.1   Checklist Definition, Types, and Examples

So what is a checklist? A checklist is a list of questions to provide reviewers with hints and recommendations for finding defects during the examination of software artifacts. Since a question can be rephrased as an imperative sentence, the checklist does not have to be composed of questions only. The questions or imperative sentences in the checklist draw reviewers' attention to defect-prone areas based on historical data. A checklist may also serve other purposes. For example, it can be used to ensure important areas are covered by the artifact under review.

Checklists can be classified into two groups (Tian, 2005): property-based checklists and artifact-based checklists. Checklists for coding standards and guidelines, standard or process conformance, etc. are property-based. Checklists for requirements specifications, design documents, code files, or test cases are artifact-based. Checklists for requirements specifications and design documents may contain items to ensure correctness, consistency, and completeness of the requirements or design, while the checklists for code review may include items for generally accepted programming practices and for particular programming languages.

Panel 3-1 shows a partial checklist for a requirements review. Note each checklist item is an imperative sentence. When a reader is reviewing a requirements specification document, he or she can check each requirement against individual items on this checklist.

PANEL 3-1: A SAMPLE (PARTIAL) CHECKLIST FOR REQUIREMENTS REVIEW

1. Requirements specifications shall be testable.

2. Requirements specifications shall not conflict with other requirements specifications.

3. Conditional requirements specifications shall cover all cases.

4. Numerical values in requirements specifications shall include physical units if applicable.

Panel 3-2 shows a sample checklist for code review. Here each checklist item is a question. The checklist for code review tends to be big and the items can be grouped into different areas of concern such as control, input/output, performance, etc. For object-oriented code reading, the areas of concern can be aligned with the features of object-oriented programming, such as encapsulation, inheritance, and polymorphism.

PANEL 3-2: A SAMPLE (PARTIAL) CHECKLIST FOR CODE REVIEW

1. Have resources (e.g., memory, file descriptor, database connection) been properly freed?

2. Are shared variables protected/thread-safe?

3. Is logging implemented?

4. Are comments updated and consistent with the code?

5. Is data unnecessarily copied, saved, or reloaded?

6. Is the number of cores checked before spawning threads?

Checklists are typically developed based on the analysis of past team defects in the same or different projects. They can also be based on others' experience, but customized for one's project team. Checklists can be tailored to an individual as well. Individuals can have a personal defect checklist that compiles the problematic areas in which the individual tends to make mistakes. The Personal Software Process prescribes the use of such a personal checklist (Humphrey, 1997).

Compared to ad hoc reading, checklist-based reading reduces the variability of reading results, i.e., the results are less dependent on the reviewers' skills, knowledge, and experience. It also ensures coverage of important areas and is thus effective at detecting omissions. As recent research suggests, in addition to supporting defect detection, checklist-based reading improves software understanding and comprehension, which makes the subsequent software modification easier (McMeekin et al., 2008).

As the Paradox of Structure suggests, checklist-based reading might detect the defects of particular types covered by the checklist, i.e., those previously encountered from which the checklist was created. Therefore insidious defects, which require deep understanding of the artifacts, are often missed. The other disadvantages of checklist-based reading are related to the checklist itself. The checklist often includes generic items that may not be applicable to the project or the artifact. A lengthy checklist may overwhelm readers. The "best practices of checklists" discussed later can remediate the issues with generic and lengthy checklists.

3.3.2 Checklists with Guidance

Checklist-based software reading is considered semi-structured, as it does not tell the reader how to use the checklist and there is little verification that the reader actually conducts an analysis relating to checklist items. To remedy this shortcoming, an active guidance can be added to the traditional checklist-based reading (Winkler et al., 2005).

Winkler et al. focused on design document inspection. The readers are given a tailored checklist that provides active guidance. The specific checklist leads the reader through the inspection process. The active guidance to be used with a checklist is shown in Panel 3-3 (adapted from Winkler et al. [2005]).

PANEL 3-3: AN ACTIVE GUIDANCE USED WITH CHECKLIST-BASED READING

1. Analyze requirements and system functions in the requirements document.

2. Prioritize the correlations between requirements and system function according to the reader's own knowledge of the application domain.

3. Trace the requirements and functions in the design document according to their priorities or importance.

4. Report any differences as defects.

5. Pick the next most important requirement and repeat steps 3 and 4, until done.

This checklist with active guidance promotes a deep understanding of the specification document, the system requirements, and system functions, which enables the readers to uncover more defects in the design document. It also allows the reader to focus on more important requirements due to the prioritization performed before the start of the inspection. Thus it uncovers crucial defects.

Alternatively, guidance on how to use a checklist can be implicitly built into the checklist itself. Dunsmore et al. (2002) compiled a checklist for object-oriented code reading. They took into account the structure of object-oriented code and deliberately ordered the checklist questions in such a way as to support readers in building up a deep understanding of the code under review. Their checklist has three ordered sections. Each section has a number of ordered groups, and each group has a list of ordered questions. Their checklist is adapted in Table 3-1. It has three sections: the class section, the method section, and the final section. The class section is about inheritance and constructor issues. The method section is concerned with issues related to methods, such as data and object referencing, messaging, and method behavior. The final section is on method overriding.

Table 3-1. *A Checklist for Object-Oriented Code Reading (adapted from Dunsmore et al. [2002])*

Section	Feature	Checklist item
For each class	Inheritance	Q1. Is all inheritance required by the design implemented in the class?
		Q2. Is the inheritance appropriate?
	Constructor	Q3. Are all instance variables initialized with meaningful values?
		Q4. If a call to base class is required in the constructor, is it present?
For each method	Data referencing	Q5. Are all parameters used within a method?
		Q6. Are the correct class constants used?
		Q7. Are indices of data structures operating within the correct boundaries?
	Object messaging	Q8. Is the correct method being called on the correct object?
		Q9. Are the correct values passed as parameters in the correct order?
	Object referencing	Q10. Should a reference to an object be used instead of a distinct copy?
	Selection and iteration	Q11. Are all relational and logical operators sufficient and correct?
		Q12. Is the correct sequence of code executed for any conditional outcome?
		Q13. Is the use of an iterator or loop appropriate when destructive operations are occurring on a collection?
	Method behavior	Q14. Are all assignment and state changes made correctly?
		Q15. For each return statement, is the value returned and its type correct?
		Q16. Does the method match the specification?
For each class	Method overriding	Q17. If inherited methods need to behave differently, are they overridden?
		Q18. Are all uses of method overriding correct?

27

The purposely structured checklist accomplishes two objectives: "where to look" and "how to detect." "Where to look" is related to the potential problem areas and is supported by the list of sections and features. The "how to detect" part is supported by the checklist questions. As the readers navigate through the different groups of questions, they successively move from a high-level view to a more detailed level view. At the end, the readers can readily conclude whether the method implementation code matches the specification (Q16).

3.3.3   Best Practices of Checklists

Over the years, people have come up with a few heuristics on what makes good checklists and what to avoid in checklists (Brykczynski, 1999). We call this general advice "the best practices of checklists":

- Checklists should be periodically revised based on historical data to include new items and remove outdated items. If the checklists are updated regularly, the reviewers may be more likely to read and use the checklists. If the checklists are updated to reflect the most common issues, more likely it will help reviewers in finding defects.

- Checklists should be concise and fit on one page. A reviewer is less likely to flip through multiple pages. The single-paged checklist can be hung on the office wall or put on the desk close to where the reviewer is examining the software artifact.

- Checklist items should not be too general. A general item is hard to apply or subject to varying interpretation.

- Checklist items should not be used for conventions which are better checked or enforced with software tools.

3.3.4   Empirical Experiences

Checklists have been used in software reading since Fagan (1976) reported the Fagan Inspection. They were advocated by many authors, e.g., Gilb and Graham (1993) and Clements et al. (2011). Checklist-based reading as well as ad hoc reading is frequently chosen as a baseline, and other newly proposed reading techniques are compared to them. Later chapters include many examples. Here we selectively discuss the results of a few empirical studies.

Winkler et al. (2005) compared the traditional checklist-based reading and checklist-based reading with guidance. Their experimental subjects were software engineering students. Defects were seeded into the design document, with three levels of severity: critical, major, and minor. They reported that checklist-based reading with guidance has a slightly longer preparation time but a shorter inspection time. When both preparation and inspection times were considered, the total times were not significantly different (although the total time of the checklist with guidance was slightly shorter). The difference was notable in the number of uncovered defects. The checklist with guidance technique uncovered more defects in all three levels of severity. It also registered less false positive defects.

Dunsmore et al. (2002) compared the deliberately designed checklist for object-oriented code reading with a few other reading techniques. In short, they found that the checklist-based reading is the most effective reading technique for object-oriented systems. The details can be found in Chapter 7, Code Reading Techniques.

Rong and colleagues (2014) reported a case study of code reading techniques in a small-sized software company. Novice software inspectors used both ad hoc reading and checklist-based reading to read source code of 20 modules. They observed that readers using the checklist tended to have a slower reading speed but discovered more defects.

The content of the checklists is accessible to both the authors of the artifact and the readers. Thus the authors can use the checklists to uncover the defects themselves before sending the artifact out for review. All the empirical studies mentioned previously ignored this fact when the checklists were used in practice. The effectiveness of checklist-based reading largely depends on the content of the checklists.

3.4 Differential Reading

Many software reading techniques assume that the reader will read the entire document, be it a requirements specification, design document, source code file, or test case. As a matter of fact, there are a few situations where developers typically deal with the difference between the existing software artifact and the one that is being modified:

- Software applications are frequently released incrementally via different projects. New features and defect fixes are added in a latter release. Many software artifacts including requirements, design, code implementation, and testing can be reused. New requirements, design, code, and test cases are typically embedded in the existing documents.

- Even for software applications that are started from scratch, an iterative and incremental development process may be adopted. New features and defect fixes are implemented in a latter iteration or sprint. Along the way, documentations are also written, revised, expanded, and reviewed incrementally.

- Regardless of how the project is structured and what development process is used, a software artifact is reviewed, a rework might be required, and the updated document might be subject to re-review again.

In all those situations, there are at least two versions of the software artifacts available. It is not worthwhile for the reader to read the entire document from beginning to end each time, particularly if the reader is already familiar with the previous versions.

There is no published reading technique to deal with the situations above. We adopt the instructions in Panel 3-4, so that the reader can focus on the changes and assess whether those changes meet the intentions without negative side effects. We call it differential reading, as it draws readers' attention to the part of changes and focuses the changes in the context. Don't be deceived by the amount of changes, however. For source code, a simple innocent change may have significant ramifications. Mernhart et al. (2010) reported their positive experience on a continuous differential-based method and tool for code reviews in agile software development.

There are many tools to highlight the changes in a document. Microsoft Word is frequently used to capture requirements and describe designs. To keep track of changes across different revisions of the document, one can enable "Track Changes". There are many tools to track the source code changes. For example, the Subversion client TortoiseSVN is integrated with the Windows Explore and the Diff command from the context menu can highlight the code change against the repository.

We illustrate one differential reading example below. The C# code reads in a script file, replaces some strings with other strings in each line, and writes the replaced script to a new file. The strings and the strings to replace them are predefined and read in from a file. However, it was noticed recently that some strings were replaced incorrectly. This happened when the prefix of a long string was mistakenly replaced first. The source code was modified in three places to fix the problem. The first place is simply to define a string list to store the sortedKeys (code not shown). Figure 3-1 shows the second section of code where the change happened. The top shows the old file and the bottom displays the new file. New code was added in the new file from line 52 to line 55. The code simply gets the list of strings and sorts them in reverse order. The comment explains why it is done.

PANEL 3-4: INSTRUCTIONS FOR DIFFERENTIAL READING

1. Get familiar with the existing software artifact if not already.

2. Understand what drives the modification of the existing document, be it new features, defect fixing, or some other nature.

3. Use a diff tool to highlight what has been changed in the newly updated document.

   a. Pick a block of changes to focus on and read the surrounding text where the changes are part of.

   b. Pay attention to all change types: addition, deletion, and modification.

   c. If the amount of change is significant, consider it new and use any reading techniques available to you or agreed upon by the team.

   d. If the amount of change is not significant:

      i. Check whether the change is consistent with the change driver, the assumptions or styles the document already took, etc. If not, log as a defect.

      ii. Check if there are any side effects. If there is a side effect, log as a defect.

4. Repeat step 3 until all changes have been read and analyzed.

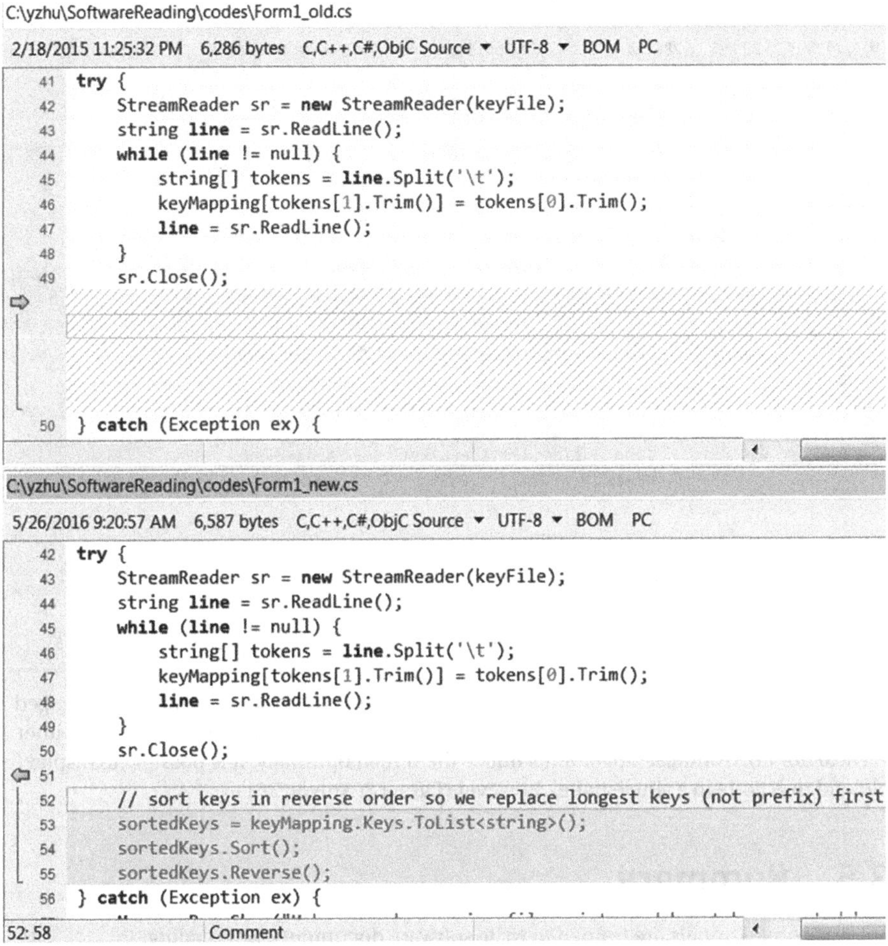

C:\yzhu\SoftwareReading\codes\Form1_old.cs

2/18/2015 11:25:32 PM   6,286 bytes   C,C++,C#,ObjC Source ▾   UTF-8 ▾   BOM   PC

```
41   try {
42       StreamReader sr = new StreamReader(keyFile);
43       string line = sr.ReadLine();
44       while (line != null) {
45           string[] tokens = line.Split('\t');
46           keyMapping[tokens[1].Trim()] = tokens[0].Trim();
47           line = sr.ReadLine();
48       }
49       sr.Close();



50   } catch (Exception ex) {
```

C:\yzhu\SoftwareReading\codes\Form1_new.cs

5/26/2016 9:20:57 AM   6,587 bytes   C,C++,C#,ObjC Source ▾   UTF-8 ▾   BOM   PC

```
42   try {
43       StreamReader sr = new StreamReader(keyFile);
44       string line = sr.ReadLine();
45       while (line != null) {
46           string[] tokens = line.Split('\t');
47           keyMapping[tokens[1].Trim()] = tokens[0].Trim();
48           line = sr.ReadLine();
49       }
50       sr.Close();
51
52       // sort keys in reverse order so we replace longest keys (not prefix) first
53       sortedKeys = keyMapping.Keys.ToList<string>();
54       sortedKeys.Sort();
55       sortedKeys.Reverse();
56   } catch (Exception ex) {
```

52: 58   Comment   ◀

Figure 3-1. Code difference (part 1) in updated file to illustrate the differential reading

Figure 3-2 shows the third and last section where the code was changed. Inside the loop in which the foreach clause is embedded, lines are processed sequentially. The original string and the string to replace it are maintained in the dictionary (keyMapping). The old code simply loops over every possible word in the dictionary, checks if it appears in the line, and replaces it if it does. The modified code however, loops over reversely sorted words. Based on the reading and understanding of the code, the modified code seems working as intended.

C:\yzhu\SoftwareReading\codes\Form1_old.cs

2/18/2015 11:25:32 PM   6,286 bytes   C,C++,C#,ObjC Source ▾   UTF-8 ▾   BOM   PC

```
116
117    foreach (var kvp in keyMapping) {
118        if (line.Contains(kvp.Key)) {
119            line = line.Replace(kvp.Key, kvp.Value);
120            break;
121        }
122    }
123    sw.WriteLine(line);
```

C:\yzhu\SoftwareReading\codes\Form1_new.cs

5/26/2016 9:20:57 AM   6,587 bytes   C,C++,C#,ObjC Source ▾   UTF-8 ▾   BOM   PC

```
122
123    foreach (string mykey in sortedKeys) {
124        if (line.Contains(mykey)) {
125            line = line.Replace(mykey, keyMapping[mykey]);
126            break;
127        }
128    }
129    sw.WriteLine(line);
52: 58                    Comment
```

Figure 3-2. *Code difference (part 2) in updated file to illustrate the differential reading.*

In this example, the old and new code is displayed in two panels, which are arranged vertically for display purpose here. Two panels can also be arranged horizontally. Neither vertical nor horizontal arrangements utilize the screen optimally. It is possible to display old and new code in a single panel, however (Lanna & Amyot, 2011).

3.5   Summary

Software professionals are trained to write software documents. But reading, understanding, analyzing, assessing quality, and utilizing the software document are equally important. This chapter defines software reading and software reading techniques and classifies the software reading techniques based on their characteristics. This chapter then discusses ad hoc reading, checklist-based reading, and differential reading, which can be applied to any software artifacts. Due to its long history, checklist-based reading has a few variations and the community accumulated some heuristics on checklist best practices. Ad hoc reading and checklist-based reading are the two most practiced reading techniques. According to a recent industry survey (Ciolkowski et al., 2003), ad hoc reading is used in 35% of the software reviews and checklist-based reading is used in 50% of the reviews. Ten percent of the reviews use some specific or advanced reading techniques and the remaining 5% use simulation or other techniques. Ad hoc and checklist-based reading techniques are also frequently chosen as a baseline and other reading techniques are compared to them. Next chapter discusses advanced reading techniques, scenario-based reading.

3.6   References

(Basili, 1996) V. Basili, G. Caldiera, F. Lanubile, and F. Shull, Studies on reading techniques, In Proceedings of the Twenty-First Annual Software Engineering Workshop, SEL-96-002, pp.59-65, 1996.

(Brykczynski, 1999) B. Brykczynski, A survey of software inspection checklists, Software Engineering Notes, vol.24, no.1, pp.82-89, 1999.

(Ciolkowski, 2003) M. Ciolkowski, O. Laitenberger, and S. Biffl, Software reviews: the state of the practice, IEEE Software, vol.20, no.6, pp.46-51, 2003.

(Clements, 2011) P. Clements, F. Bachmann, L. Bass, D. Garlan, J. Ivers, R. Little, P. Merson, R. Nord, and J. Stafford, Documenting Software Architectures: Views and Beyond, 2nd ed., Addison-Wesley, 2011.

(Dunsmore, 2002) A. Dunsmore, M. Roper, and M. Wood, Further investigations into the development and evaluation of reading techniques for object-oriented code inspection, Proceedings of the 24th International Conference on Software Engineering, pp.47-57, 2002.

(Fagan, 1976) M.E. Fagan, Design and code inspections to reduce errors in program development, IBM Systems Journal, vol.15, no.3, pp.182-211, 1976.

(Gilb, 1993) T. Gilb and D. Graham, Software Inspection, Addison-Wesley, 1993.

(Hatton, 2008) L. Hatton, Testing the value of checklists in code inspections, IEEE Software, vol.25, no.4, pp.82-88, 2008.

(Humphrey, 1997) W.S. Humphrey, Introduction to the Personal Software Process, Addison-Wesley Publishing Company, 1997.

(Jablokow, 2003) K.W. Jablokow, Systems, man, and the paradox of structure, IEEE International Conference on Systems, Man and Cybernetics, vol.3, pp.2374-2380, 2003.

(Johnson, 1998) P.M. Johnson and D. Tjahjono, Does every inspection really need a meeting? Empirical Software Engineering, vol.3, pp.9-35, 1998.

(Kollanus, 2009) S. Kollanus and J. Koskinen, Survey of software inspection research, The Open Software Engineering Journal, vol.3, pp.15-34, 2009.

(Lanna, 2011) M. Lanna and D. Amyot, Spotting the difference, Software: Practice and Experience, vol.41, no.6, pp.607-622, 2011.

(McMeekin, 2008) D.A. McMeekin, B.R. von Konsky, E. Chang, and D.J.A. Cooper, Checklist based reading's influence on a developer's understanding, 19th Australian Conference on Software Engineering, pp.489-496, 2008.

(Mernhart, 2010) M. Mernhart, A. Mauczka, and T. Grechenig, Adopting code reviews for agile software development, IEEE Agile Conference, pp.44-47, 2010.

(Porter, 1994) A.A. Porter and L.G. Votta, An experiment to assess different defect detection methods for software requirements inspections, in Proceedings of the 16th International Conference on Software Engineering, pp.103-112, 1994.

(Rong, 2014) G. Rong, H. Zhang, and D. Shao, Investigating code reading techniques for novice inspectors: an industrial case study, Proceedings of the 18th International Conference on Evaluation and Assessment in Software Engineering (EASE'14), Article No.33, 2014.

(Shull, 2002) F. Shull, Software reading techniques, in Encyclopedia of Software Engineering, John Wiley and Sons, 2002 (http://onlinelibrary.wiley.com/doi/10.1002/0471028959.sof273/abstract, accessed on Dec. 17, 2015).

(Tian, 2005) J. Tian, Software Quality Engineering: testing, quality assurance, and quantifiable improvement, IEEE Computer Society Press, 2005.

(Votta, 1993) L.G. Votta Jr., Does every inspection need a meeting? Proceedings of the ACM SIGSOFT Symposium on Foundations of Software Engineering, pp.107-114, 1993.

(Winkler, 2005) D. Winkler, S. Biffl, and B. Thurnher, Investigating the impact of active guidance on design inspection, LNCS 3547, pp.458-473, 2005.

CHAPTER 4

Scenario-Based Reading Techniques

In the last chapter we discussed basic reading techniques such as ad hoc reading and checklist-based reading. Those are the most frequently used reading techniques in industry software reviews (Ciolkowski et al., 2003). This chapter discusses recent developments of software reading techniques and focuses on the family of reading techniques called scenario-based reading.

4.1   Principles of Scenario-Based Reading

Scenario-based reading was developed by Porter and Votta (1994), and their paper triggered an active research on software reading techniques. Their method was later renamed "defect-based reading" and the term "scenario-based reading" was reserved for a group of reading techniques that use different ways to decompose reading scenarios. The family of scenario-based reading techniques includes defect-based reading, perspective-based reading, etc. Defect-based reading concentrates on specific defect classes and perspective-based reading focuses on viewpoints of consumers of a document. Defect-based reading was originally employed for requirements inspection but could be applied to other software artifacts as well.

Scenario-based reading was motivated by the ideas behind the active design review proposed by Parnas and Weiss (1985). In an active design review, reviewers are selected based on their expertise. Each reviewer is given a specific area to focus on and required to answer specifically designed questions that can only be answered after a critical reading and analysis of the design, which solves the issue of passive participation. Scenario-based reading is based on operational scenarios that give specific guidance to readers. The guidance can be a set of questions, an assignment, or explicit instructions on how to conduct reviews and look for defects. To improve effectiveness, the overlap of scenario assignments shall be minimized. Because of detailed instructions on reading and defect detection, this group of reading techniques is considered systematic.

The working of scenario-based reading can be best depicted by the diagram in Figure 4-1, where the rectangle shape represents a software artifact to be reviewed, and both open and filled circles with various sizes represent different kinds of defects in the artifact. Two reading techniques are schematically illustrated in Figure 4-1.

© Yang-Ming Zhu 2016

Y.-M. Zhu, *Software Reading Techniques*, DOI 10.1007/978-1-4842-2346-8_4

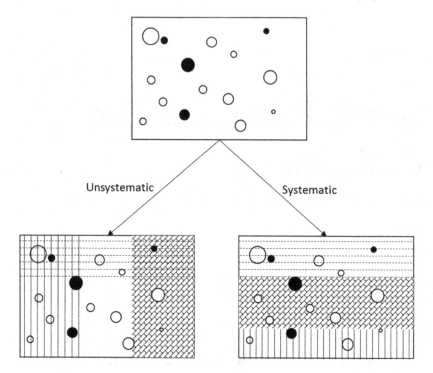

Figure 4-1. *Comparison of unsystematic and systematic (scenario-based) reading (adapted from Porter & Votta [1994])*

To the left of Figure 4-1 is an unsystematic reading, where one or more readers scan through the document and look for defects, which are shaded as vertical, horizontal, or slanted lines. There are at least two problems with that approach owning to its unsystematic nature: (a) there are overlaps on the portions covered by different readers, and (b) there are regions that are not covered by any reader. To the right is a systematic reading, where different readers are purposely selected to exam the software artifact, based on their individual expertise. They are also given specific instructions on where and how to detect defects. These two ensure that there will be no or minimal overlaps among what they will cover and the entire document is covered. Systematic approaches with specific responsibilities improve coordination and reduce gaps, which increases the overall defect detection effectiveness of review.

The scenario used here refers to a process-driven or operational scenario, not to be confused with scenarios in the use-case context. It is expressed in the form of algorithms that readers can apply to traverse a document with a particular emphasis. In practice several scenarios must be combined to provide an adequate coverage of a document, since each scenario is focused, detailed, and specific to a particular viewpoint (Basili et al., 1996).

Before analyzing and detecting defects in a document, one must understand the document first. In cognitive science, comprehension is often characterized as the construction of a mental model that represents the objects and relationships in the text document (Schulte et al., 2010). An operational scenario has a set of activities to help a reader build a model of the software artifact and a set of review questions related to the model. The model is simply an abstraction of the software artifact under review. In the defect-based reading, the model can be different types of defects the document may have. In the perspective-based reading, if the reader reads the code from a tester point of view, the model can be related to how testing can be performed. While the reader builds a model and answers the questions based on the analysis of the model with a particular emphasis, he or she can note down any anomaly and log defects. To minimize the potential reading overlap, scenarios shall be orthogonal to each other. One team member is responsible for one scenario and multiple members provide complete coverage. The findings of individual team members are aggregated via meeting or non-meeting, which depends on the inspection process bestowed by the organization. The choice of model or abstraction and the types of questions depend on artifacts, the organization's problem history, or the objectives of reading.

Compared with other reading techniques such as ad hoc or checklist-based reading, the scenario-based reading techniques have the following benefits (Shull et al., 2000):

- *Systematic*: Specific steps for individual reading are well-defined.

- *Focused*: Different readers focus on distinct aspects of the document.

- *Allow controlled improvement*: Based on experience and feedback, one can identify and improve specific aspects of reading techniques.

- *Customizable*: Organizations can customize reading techniques to a specific project or organization setting.

- *Allow training*: One can use reading techniques to train oneself in applying the techniques.

4.2 Defect-Based Reading

Defect-based reading is the first proposed reading technique in the family of scenario-based reading and focused on detecting specific types of defects. The main idea is that if each reader uses different but systematic techniques to search for different, specific classes of defects, he or she and the whole team will have a better chance to detect defects effectively than readers applying ad hoc reading or checklist-based reading (Porter et al., 1995). In this defect-based software reading, each reader is given specific steps to discover a particular class of defects. Each reader's role or responsibility is specific and narrowly defined, such as ensuring appropriate use of hardware interfaces, identifying untestable requirements, or checking conformance to coding standards and guidelines. The defect-based reading technique has been applied to detecting defects in software requirements specifications (SRS) and we discuss it in the context of SRS reading.

4.2.1 Taxonomy of Defects in Requirements Specifications

Defects in SRS can be divided into two broad types: omission and commission (Porter et al., 1995). An omission defect means important information is missing from the SRS, while a commission type defect means incorrect, redundant, ambiguous, or conflicting information is presented in the SRS. Depending on what is missing, the omission type can be further divided into four groups:

- *Missing functionality*: The specification of the internal operational behavior of the system is not included in the SRS.

- *Missing performance*: The performance specification is not present in the SRS or is not acceptable by end users in an acceptance testing.

- *Missing environment*: The environment in which the system will be operated is not specified or is specified incompletely in the SRS, including infrastructure, middleware, hardware, software, database, personnel, and so on.

- *Missing interface*: The interfaces through which the system interacts and interoperates with outside or communication mechanisms or protocols through which the system exchanges data with outside is not included in the SRS.

The commission type of defects also has four subcategories: ambiguous information, inconsistent information, incorrect or extra functionality, and wrong section:

- *Ambiguous information*: Technical terms, phrases, or anything essential for readers to correctly understand and interpret the SRS is undefined or defined in such a way to cause misunderstanding or misinterpretation.

- *Inconsistent information*: Information in different parts of the SRS contradicts each other directly or indirectly, or actions or behaviors cannot both be correct or carried out by the system.

- *Incorrect fact*: Specifications in the SRS cannot be true in the given context.

- *Wrong section*: The SRS is poorly organized or the specification is put in a wrong section of the SRS.

There are other defect taxonomies. IEEE Std. 1028-2008 categorizes anomaly (defects) as missing, extra (superfluous), ambiguous, inconsistent, not conforming to standards, risk-prone, incorrect, unachievable, and editorial (IEEE 2008). In the recent survey, Walia and Carver (2009) attributed the defects to their sources, i.e., people, process, and documentation.

4.2.2 Defect-Based Reading Techniques

When readers are assigned to review and detect defects in a software artifact, they can have the same general responsibilities, e.g., detect as many defects as they can, and their reading activities are not coordinated. Alternatively, in a coordinated team, readers can have separate and different responsibilities. As the active design review suggests, individual readers can be more effective if they are assigned specific responsibilities and provided systematic techniques to meet those responsibilities (Parnas & Weiss, 1985). The defect-based reading technique is motivated by the ideas behind the active design review. In this reading technique, a collection of procedures (operational scenarios) for detecting particular classes of defects is developed. Each reader executes one single scenario, and multiple readers are coordinated to improve the coverage while minimizing the overlap (Porter et al., 1995).

One way to come up with operational scenarios is to make use of the defect taxonomy, as discussed by Porter and his colleagues (1995). The general defect taxonomy discussed earlier can be given to ad hoc readers and used to define their responsibilities. To support checklist-based reading, detailed and concrete questions as checklist items can be developed under each defect classes. The checklist is thus a refinement of the taxonomy. Those questions can be motivated by industrial checklists. For example, to detect defects related to inconsistent information, one can have following checklist items (Porter et al., 1995):

- Are the requirements mutually consistent?

- Are the functional requirements consistent with the system overview?

- Are the functional requirements consistent with the operating environment?

The actual defect types, groups, and classes shall depend on the software artifact under concern and be based on the organizational experience. Checklist items shall be customized to detect those defects accordingly. Since the checklist is derived from the defect taxonomy, checklist responsibilities are a subset of the ad hoc responsibilities.

Scenarios for defect-based reading are further derived from the checklist by substituting the checklist items with procedures designed to implement them. Hence, the responsibilities of defect-based reading is a subset of checklist-based reading. If defect-based reading scenarios cover all checklist items, defect-based reading and checklist-based reading can detect the same kinds of defects. The diagram in Figure 4-2 shows the relationship among the ad hoc, checklist-based, and defect-based reading techniques. The horizontal axis labels the reading technique and denotes the increased degrees of details in reading procedures. As the reading technique becomes more sophisticated (moving to the right), the defect coverage decreases. The reading responsibilities and the classes of defects targeted for the latter reading technique are the subset of the former reading techniques (moving to the left).

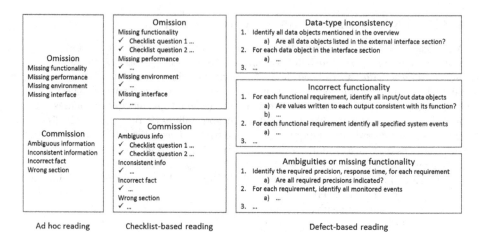

Figure 4-2. *The relationship among ad hoc reading, checklist-based reading, and defect-based reading (adapted from Porter et al. [1995])*

Porter et al. (1995) developed three defect detection scenarios for their defect-based reading. Each scenario was designed for a specific subset of checklist items. Those scenarios were intended to detect defects in areas of data type inconsistency, incorrect functionality, and ambiguous or missing functionality. According to their estimate, those scenarios cover about 50% of the defects present in the SRS. Their Incorrect Functionality Scenario is reproduced in Panel 4-1: Defect-Based Reading (Incorrect Functionality Scenario), and interested readers can refer to their original paper for the other two reading scenarios.

PANEL 4-1: DEFECT-BASED READING (INCORRECT FUNCTIONALITY SCENARIO)

1. For each functional requirement, identify all input and output data objects.

    a. Are all values written to each output data object consistent with its intended function?

    b. Identify at least one function that uses each output data object.

2. For each functional requirement, identify all specified system events.

    a. Is the specification of these events consistent with their intended interpretation?

3. Develop an invariant for each system mode or state, i.e., under what conditions must the system exit or remain in a given mode.

   a. Can the system's initial conditions fail to satisfy the initial mode's invariant?

   b. Identify a sequence of events that allows the system to enter a mode without satisfying the mode's invariant.

   c. Identify a sequence of events that allows the system to enter a mode but never leave.

The operational scenario leads a reader through the SRS and gives the reader instructions where and how to find defects. For example, in (1), "where" would be the input and output data object related to a functional requirement, and "how" is to check if all values generated for the output data object is consistent with its intended function and check whether the output data object is used by some functions. From this scenario, one can clearly see the influence of active design review. It turns a passive reader into an active reader (e.g., step 3) and therefore improves readers' effectiveness.

Defect-based reading is a systematic technique that focuses the readers on detecting the specific class of defects that the scenario targets, providing a mechanism to focus the reading according to project or organizational objectives. As scenarios are typically derived from checklist items, the technique suffers the similar drawbacks as checklist-based reading. For maximal coverage of defects, multiple scenarios have to be defined, which could be an elaborated process. In practice, defect-based reading has to be applied in combination with other reading techniques so that defects not covered by the defect scenarios can still be detected.

Defect-based reading has been applied to requirements reading. In theory, it can be applied to other artifacts. There are no other applications reported yet.

4.2.3 Empirical Experiences

Porter et al. (1994; 1995) used graduate students in computer science in their experiments to test the effectiveness of defect-based reading by comparing it with ad hoc reading and checklist-based reading. To some degree, they replicated and expanded their experiment and came to the same conclusion. The taxonomy was provided to all readers, but ad hoc readers were not given further instructions. The checklist and the scenarios were developed in the way discussed earlier. They concluded that defect-based reading had the highest defect detection rate (about 35% improvement over the other two reading techniques), followed by ad hoc reading, and checklist-based reading had the lowest effectiveness. Further analysis confirmed that defect-based scenario readers were more effective than ad hoc and checklist readers at finding defects the scenario was designed to detect, and all readers were equally effective at detecting other defects not targeted by scenarios. Scenarios helped readers focus on specific defect types, and they didn't compromise readers' ability to detect other defect types not covered by scenarios. Porter and Votta (1998) replicated the same experiment using industrial professionals and reported the similar results, although the performances of students and professionals were different.

Porter et al. studies were replicated by other researchers (Fusaro et al., 1997; Miller et al., 1998; Sandahl et al., 1998). However, the results were not consistent with the original findings, mainly defect-based reading was not significantly better than other ad hoc and checklist-based readings. Hayes used meta-analytic (analysis of analyses) methods to synthesize the series of replicated experiments with seemingly contradictory results (Hayes, 1999). He suggested that the differences might be caused by subjects' familiarity with the formal notation used in the SRS and with the software domains used in the experiment (e.g., cars with cruise control were popular in the United States but not in the Europe).

4.3 Perspective-Based Reading

Perspective-based reading was developed by Basili et al. (1996). It provides a set of operational scenarios. Each reader reads a software artifact under review using one of the scenarios from a particular perspective, and the combination of different perspectives yields a better coverage of the document. It was originally applied to requirements documents but subsequently applied to high-level designs, source code, and user interface. Perspective-based reading in fact includes a family of reading techniques. In this section we present perspective-based reading in its generic form first, then discuss specifics when the technique is applied to different types of software artifacts. Finally we shed light on why the reading techniques are effective in practice.

4.3.1 A Generic Perspective-Based Reading

Software artifacts are created with various purposes. It is important to ask their stakeholders to read and assess if the documents meet their needs and quality expectation, from a particular point of view, which is called perspective. Perspective-based reading focuses on a point of view or needs of the main customers of a document. Each reader reads from their respective perspective with a narrowly defined focused view, which leads to an in-depth analysis of potential defects or anomalies in the document. The union of multiple perspectives provides an extensive coverage of the document so that no defects will be missed.

Defect reports from individual readings are aggregated at the end of reading. It is not necessarily true that we select one reader for each perspective. How many readers are assigned to a given perspective depends on the organizational and project context. For example, if more omission defects are expected in a requirements specification, one may assign more readers to the user role, since a user perspective offers better opportunity for exposing omission defects. If there are not enough resources available, one reader may be assigned to multiple roles and he or she can simulate each perspective in turn.

When read with a particular perspective, defects that a perspective is targeting at would have a higher probability to be detected, while other defects not targeted by the perspective might have a lower probability to be detected. Thus an individual using perspective-based reading may not be necessarily more effective and efficient than one using other reading techniques. Collectively on the team level, perspective-based reading could be more effective and efficient as each perspective detects different kinds of defects.

The idea of perspective-based reading is not completely new, however. It synthesizes ideas that have already been applied in software inspection, but have never been worked out in great detail. The influence of the active design review was already mentioned. Fagan (1976) stated that the code should be inspected by its tester. When reporting AT&T experience on in-process inspection, Fowler (1986) stated, "[E]ach meeting participant takes a particular point of view when examining the workproduct." Graden et al. (1986) also reported that when collecting the software inspection data, each participant must denote the perspective (customer, requirements, design, test, maintenance) by which they have evaluated the deliverable.

4.3.1.1   Reading Scenarios and Template

Perspective-based reading has a set of operational scenarios that provide reading guidance to readers. In an ideal case, those scenarios shall have a minimal overlap in defects detection, which is very hard to achieve in practice (Regnell et al., 2000). What scenarios to provide to readers depends on many factors such as artifact types, organization's history on defects, as well as organizational objectives of software reviews.

The scenarios are developed using a scenario template, which has three sections:

- *Introduction*: The introduction section explains the stakeholder's interests in the artifact.

- *Instruction*: The instruction section provides guidance regarding how to read and extract relevant information from artifacts or from the descriptions of artifacts and to optionally create other artifacts such as test cases from a tester's perspective or a high-level design from a designer's perspective. It helps a reader focus on the most relevant information and actively work with the document to gain a deep understanding of it.

- *Question*: The question section is for reviewers to answer by following the instructions above. Questions are derived from past defect classes.

It shall be noted that to review software artifacts, one can ask real stakeholders and experts to review. One can also ask other readers to review, who will mimic real stakeholders' perspective. For the latter case, the introduction section of a scenario is important to set up the scope and expectation. Even when real stakeholders and experts are invited to review a document, they will appreciate the concrete guidance provided in the latter two sections of the scenario. However, people with less experience seem to follow the prescribed perspectives while people with more experience are more likely not to conform to their prescribed perspectives (Basili et al., 1996).

4.3.1.2   Developing Reading Scenarios

Scenarios play a pivotal role in perspective-based reading. How are the scenarios created from the first place? Herein this section, we provide some guidance on scenario creation based on Laitenberger and Atkinson (1999).

1. Document identification. Identify documents subject to reading. This might be a software requirements specification document, software architectural or design description including diagrams and graphical models, source code files, a test plan including detailed test cases, or a graphical user interface mockup, etc.

2. Stakeholder identification. For the identified artifacts and their descriptions, identify key stakeholders who have a vested interest in the artifacts to be reviewed. Those stakeholders can be subject matter experts, users, or maintainers. They can be the consumer of the artifacts or the producer of upstream documents from which the current documents are based. They can also be peers of the author who created the artifacts. Prioritize those stakeholders according to the potential gain from the reading activities and resource constraint.

3. Perspective understanding. For the identified key stakeholders, understand their perspectives by deciding and collecting what information and descriptions are important to them. You can interview and survey stakeholders to collect their inputs. After having understood the stakeholders, the scenario writer identifies which documents contain that information and how to identify and extract the information.

4. Introduction development. The scenario writer writes the introduction to a particular perspective and highlights stakeholders' interests in the artifacts.

5. Instruction development. The scenario writer develops the detailed instruction on how to identify and extract, step by step, the required information from the artifact or the descriptions of the artifact.

6. Questions development. The scenario writer compiles a list of questions for a reader to answer based on the extracted information and the reader's understanding of the artifact. The checklist, if available, as well as the historical defects can be a source for those questions. The writer makes sure only pertinent questions are included, i.e., those the reader could answer by reading and analyzing the documents from the given perspective.

7. Scenario review, testing, and updating. After the scenarios are written, the scenario writer should invite stakeholders to review and pilot its usage to get rid of kinks in the scenarios. The above steps shall be iterated as necessary. The scenarios shall also be kept up to date. When new defects are uncovered, or the contents and structures of the documents are changed, the scenario instruction and questions shall be updated as well.

4.3.1.3   Characteristics of Perspective-Based Reading

Perspective-based reading has been developed to satisfy a variety of goals, which are discussed below (Ciolkowski et al., 1997):

- *Adaptable*. Perspective-based reading is adaptable to particular software artifacts, being it requirements specification, design description, source code, and user interface. It is also adaptable to whatever notation used in the document. For example, the requirements might be specified using natural languages or a more formal specification language.

- *Tailorable:* Perspective-based reading is tailorable to organizational and project setting: The number of perspectives, the number of readers using a scenario, and the reading instruction and questions in a scenario are all customizable.

- *Detailed*: A reading scenario gives a reader a well-defined instruction how to traverse a document. Hence the reading process is repeatable and the effectiveness of defect detection becomes less dependent on individual's experience and expertise.

- *Focused*: A particular perspective provides particular coverage of part of the document and multiple perspectives combined provide coverage of the whole document. This gives individual reader a focus, which enables an in-depth analysis. At the same time, multiple perspectives ensure no areas are left unread.

- *Specific*: Each reader has a specific, narrowly defined responsibility, with a specific tool (scenario) to meet this responsibility. The reader knows what perspective to simulate, which scenario to use, and where and how to detect defects.

Those benefits will become more evident as we go through the reading techniques for specific types of documents in the remainder of this chapter. Perspective-based reading is not without drawbacks. The most noticeable one is the demanded effort. The improved rate of defect detection comes at the price of a higher effort on the reviewer. Basili et al. (1996) reported about 30% more effort, depending on the document under review. Much of the extra effort was spent on creating additional model and documentation, which might be required in a later stage of the development life cycle, e.g., test cases created during the requirement reading can be reused later in the testing phase

4.3.2   Perspective-Based Requirements Reading

Many researchers have applied perspective-based reading to requirements documents. In fact, it was first applied to the requirements document when the reading technique was developed. This should not be a surprise, given the importance of a requirements document in the software development process. Any problems and issues in requirements specification detected and corrected early can save a lot of time and money of the development organization, since it will reduce potential rework of design, implementation, and testing, or avoid embarrassment if the product is shipped to customers with residual defects.

4.3.2.1   Reading Scenarios for Requirements Specifications

There are many possible stakeholders of a requirements document. Basili et al. (1996) identified three key consumers of a requirements document, i.e., end user, tester, and designer. The requirements describe functionalities and performance expectations that the finished software product must meet; thus the end user is an important stakeholder. The requirements are the basis for system design and the designer must create a design that provides the functionalities with the performance constraints documented in the requirements; therefore the designer is another important stakeholder. The finished software system must be verified to be conformant to functional and performance specifications, which is typically conducted by a tester; hence the tester is yet another important stakeholder of the requirements document.

From the user's perspective, requirements must be complete and correct and provide necessary system functionality. From the tester's perspective, requirements must be testable with unambiguity so that the tester can construct test cases. From the designer's perspective, requirements must have enough details with accuracy so that the designer can design major system components. Failing to satisfy any of the above needs amounts to a requirement defect. Operational scenarios must be developed for the perspectives of the end user, tester, and developer.

Given the overarching impact of a requirements specification, it often involves more inspectors or readers than other types of software artifacts do. Other stakeholders and their perspectives might be important or even critical, depending on a particular environment. For example, for the software requirements for a nuclear power plant-related system, designer, tester, user, maintainer, verifier, regulator, and contractor might be identified as key stakeholder (Lahtinen, 2011). As a nuclear power plant has a long lifetime (60 years), maintainer is a critical stakeholder as well.

One of the key ideas behind the active design review is to engage reviewers for active participation. With the same spirit, when a reader reads from a perspective, he or she is asked to create a physical model and answer questions from the same perspective based on the analysis of the model. When reading from the tester's perspective, the reader is asked to design a set of test cases and answer questions related to the activities being performed. Similarly, when reading from the developer's perspective, the reader is asked to create a high-level design, and when reading from the user's perspective, the reader can develop use cases or draft a user's manual. The exact document to generate can vary according to the reader's experience or the organization's needs. Shull et al. (2000) provided a test-based reading scenario that asked a reader to develop a test case using the equivalence partitioning technique (generating and testing the equivalent sets). Chen et al. (2002) took a step even further, where they proposed a problem-driven approach to select a method for test suite construction. The questions to answer are tied to the defects taxonomy, and additional questions can be added for newly found defect classes.

An example test-based reading scenario is show in Panel 4-2: PBR – Requirement Reading Scenario for Testers. It was adapted from Basili et al. (1996). Question 1 is more operable than a general question one might find on a checklist such as "Are all items sufficiently and unambiguously described?" and intended to detect defects of the "missing information" class. Question 2 is intended to detect defects of the "inconsistent" class. Question 4 is intended to detect defects of the "ambiguous" class. Question 5 is intended to detect defects of the "incorrect facts" class.

4.3.2.2   Empirical Experiences

Basili et al. (1996) tested their perspective-based reading techniques on requirements documents using professional software developers as subjects. The techniques were compared to the existing techniques at NASA Goddard Space Flight Center Software Engineering Laboratory. Readers were given unique roles (user, tester, and designer) when reading four requirement documents, two from NASA domain and the other two generic. They reported that perspective-based reading provided significantly better coverage of both domain-specific and generic documents. The experiment of Basili et al. was replicated and original findings were confirmed in an academic environment (Ciolkowski et al., 1997). In the replicated experiment, perspective-based reading was compared to ad hoc reading. Perspective-based reading of requirements was replicated by many other groups. However, the positive effects were not observed all the time. Regnell et al. (2000) questioned whether all the perspectives were really orthogonal and people using them found different kinds of defects. To address that, Maldonado et al. (2006) replicated the experiment with students as subjects. They confirmed that, in general, different perspectives detect different kinds of defects. They also reported that perspective-based reading didn't outperform checklist-based reading and perspective-based reading and checklist-based reading appeared to be complementary on defect detection.

PANEL 4-2: PBR – REQUIREMENT READING SCENARIO FOR TESTERS

Introduction: Perspective-based reading is built around the concept that customers of a document are at the best position to judge if the document meets their needs and quality expectation. Different customer reads the document and detects defects from their respective perspective. This reading scenario assumes a tester's perspective. From the tester's perspective, requirements must be testable and unambiguous.

Instructions: For each requirement or functional specification, create a test case to verify that the implementation satisfies the requirement. Compose test cases into a test suite. While composing the test suite, answer questions below.

Questions:

1. Do you have all information to identify the item being tested and to identify your test criteria? Can you create reasonable test cases for each item based on the criteria?

2. Is there another requirement for which you would create a similar test case but would get a contradictory result?

3. Can you be sure the test generated will output the correct value in the correct units?

4. Are there other interpretations of the requirement that the implementer might make due to the particular description of the requirement? Will this impact the test case and its oracle?

5. Does the requirement make sense based on your domain knowledge or from what is specified in the general description?

4.3.3 Perspective-Based Design Reading

Most software reading techniques target textual documents such as requirements specifications and source code files. Design documents are typically written as textual descriptions annotated with graphical models and diagrams, which is particularly true for object-oriented designs. An object-oriented approach is more popular nowadays than other paradigms such as procedure or structured programming, but it is much more complicated and error-prone in both design and implementation. This section discusses how the perspective-based reading technique can be customized to read the object-oriented designs.

4.3.3.1 Reading Scenarios for Design Documents

Unified modeling language (UML) is often used in object-oriented modeling at analysis and design levels. Use-case diagrams are used to capture the interaction with the system and the requirements of the system. Class diagrams are used to document the static structure. The dynamic behaviors can be captured using state diagrams, activity diagrams, sequence diagrams, or collaboration diagrams. The last two kinds of diagrams capture identical information from different perspectives. What UML diagrams and textual documents to generate depend on the project and team needs. Laitenberger and Atkinson (1999) suggested operation schema, class diagrams, collaboration diagrams, operation pseudocode, and data dictionary, where the operation schema is simply a method description, the operation pseudocode is the pseudocode for the method, and the data dictionary is a catalog of each modeled object with description.

We can identify the following stakeholders of a design: requirements engineer, designer, implementer, tester, and maintainer. A requirements engineer has a high interest to make sure requirements specifications have been fully and correctly considered in the design. A designer is primarily interested in the correctness of the design models and the analysis documents. An implementer wants to make sure all necessary information is provided in the design models so that he or she can realize the design. A tester wants to know what functionalities are implemented and how to develop test cases to verify the correctness of those operations. A maintainer will extend the design and implement new functionalities in the future and he or she has a vested interest if the design has an acceptable maintainability. The number of reading scenarios to develop for stakeholders depends on the organizational context, history, and objectives. Laitenberger et al. (2000) used three reading scenarios (designer, implementer, and tester), but they used four (requirements engineer, designer, tester, and maintainer) in (Laitenberger & Atkinson, 1999). Sabaliauskaite et al. (2003) used three reading scenarios (user, designer, and implementer).

Stakeholders have vested interests in different documents assembled for a design. A possible association is shown in Table 4-1. The concern of a requirements engineer is the correctness and completeness of the functional specification at the end of the analysis. Particularly, various analysis models shall be consistent. Thus the requirements engineer has a high interest in the data dictionary, method descriptions (operation schema), as well as the responsibility assigned to each class.

Table 4-1. *Stakeholders' Interests in Different Design Description Documents (Adapted from Laitenberger et al. [1999; 2000])*

	Requirements Engineer	Designer	Implementer	Tester	Maintainer
Operation schema	x	x		x	
Class diagram	x	x	x		
Collaboration diagram		x	x	x	x
Operation pseudocode			x	x	x
Data dictionary	x				

The designer concerns the correctness and completeness of the design diagrams with respect to the analysis. In terms of correctness, design diagrams shall be consistent with analysis diagrams. In terms of completeness, all elements in analysis diagrams shall be reflected in design diagrams with sufficient details. Thus he or she is interested in the operation schema, collaboration or sequence diagrams, and class diagrams. A sample design reading scenario for designer is given in Panel 4-3: PBR – Design Reading Scenario for Designers, which is adapted from Laitenberger et al. (2000). One can customize it when experimenting or adopting perspective-based reading.

PANEL 4-3: PBR – DESIGN READING SCENARIO FOR DESIGNERS

Introduction: Assume a designer's perspective when reading the design artifacts. A designer concerns the correctness and completeness of design diagrams with respect to analysis diagrams.

Instructions: Get familiar with the purpose of the system and the requirements (use cases). Locate the class diagrams, compare them with analysis diagrams, and make sure classes, attributes, methods, associations, constraints, and other abstract concepts are consistent. As design diagrams are a refinement of analysis diagrams, design diagrams sometimes contain additional elements. Locate collaboration diagrams and compare them to the corresponding operation schema, and make sure the messages, parameters and their types, and the resulting behaviors are consistent.

Questions: While following the instruction, answer questions:

1. Is there anything in analysis documents but not in design documents?

2. Are the messages appropriate and consistent from the collaboration diagrams and operation schema?

3. Are the system start-up conditions clear and correct?

4. Are there corresponding sent messages in operation schema and collaboration diagrams?

5. Is the order of messages correct in the collaboration diagram?

6. For every change of attributes, objects, states, or links in the operation schema, is there a corresponding sent message in the collaboration diagram?

7. Are there any discrepancies of functionality described in the operation schema and in the collaboration diagram?

The main responsibility of an implementer is to translate the design into code. As such, the implementer is concerned with the consistency and completeness of the design, as well as whether the design is implementable. To check for consistency, the implementer reads and detects any contradictions among design elements scattered in multiple diagrams. To check for completeness, the implementer reads and detects any missing elements from diagrams based on the analysis and design models. The implementer makes a professional judgment regarding whether the design is implementable based on project constraints, technologies and development environment, as well as other considerations. The implementer has high vested interests in the class diagram, collaboration diagram, and pseudocode. He or she will verify the messages received by an object as documented in the sequence or collaboration diagram are implemented by the class, and the collaboration diagram is consistent with the operation pseudocode.

The tester is concerned if the operations are testable. A productive approach is to walk through test cases and ensure test cases are correct with respect to the associated functions. The tester is thus interested in the operation schema and their collaboration diagram as well as pseudocode that implements the collaboration. A design reading scenario for testers is illustrated in Panel 4-4: PBR – Design Reading Scenario for Testers, which is adapted from Laitenberger et al. (2000).

We contrast this tester-based reading scenario with that for the requirements specification. Here since the internal implementation is available as revealed in the pseudocode and collaboration diagrams, white-box testing becomes feasible, i.e., one can develop test cases to cover the various branches and loops, which is not feasible when only the requirements are available.

The maintainer is concerned with the maintainability of the system. To improve the maintainability or modifiability of a system, the designer shall follow well-established design principles such as low coupling and high cohesion as well as simplicity of the design. Bass et al. (2013) have written about the tactics of improved modifiability. The proper places to check whether best practices are followed are collaboration diagrams and pseudocode.

PANEL 4-4: PBR – DESIGN READING SCENARIO FOR TESTERS

Introduction: Assume a tester's perspective when reading design artifacts. Ensure the correctness and robustness of all operations and their testability. For this perspective-based reading, test cases are used. If they don't exist yet, have them created.

Instructions: Get familiar with the requirements (use cases). Locate the operation schema and identify test cases derived from the schema. Locate the collaboration diagram associated with the operation schema. Walk through the collaboration diagram and simulate the execution of the test cases; check if the correct results are generated, all branches and paths are covered, and the resulting behavior is consistent with schema.

Questions: While following the instruction, answer questions:

1. Do the branches in the collaboration diagram match the condition outcomes in the operation schema?

2. Are all possible inputs and their combinations properly addressed in the operation schema and the pseudocode?

3. Are the effects of each collaboration diagram consistent with the corresponding operation schema?

4.3.3.2 Empirical Experiences

Laitenberger et al. (2000) compared perspective-based design reading to checklist-based reading, with practitioners (experienced students) as subjects. The software artifacts under reading were UML design documents. Their checklist was developed from scratch. Three reading perspectives were employed (designer, implementer, and tester). For both reading techniques, defects were pooled through the defect collection meeting attended by three team members. They reported that teams found more defects using perspective-based reading than using checklist-based reading and, on average, the improvement of detection effectiveness is 41%. When considering the defect detection effort, perspective-based reading was also cost-effective for the defect detection phase, the meeting phase, and the overall inspection. The readers also believed that applying perspective-based reading helped them improve their understanding of the systems.

Sabaliauskaite et al. (2003) also compared perspective-based reading and checklist-based reading of UML design documents with students as subjects. The UML diagrams include class diagrams, activity diagrams, sequence diagrams, and component diagrams. They used three reading perspectives (user, designer, and implementer). The authors concluded that defect detection effectiveness using both reading techniques was similar, but checklist-based reading was more effective for three-person simulated virtual teams.

4.3.4　Perspective-Based Code Reading

In industry practice, code documents are still the most frequently inspected software artifacts. It is thus natural to apply perspective-based reading to code. This section discusses the work in that area.

4.3.4.1　Reading Scenarios for Code Modules

Code modules subject to inspection include implementation source code files as well as their operational descriptions as specification. We can identify two main stakeholders of those artifacts: code analyst and tester (Laitenberger et al., 2001). While a code analyst is concerned if the code implements the right function, a tester is concerned if the code implements the function right.

One could certainly identify more stakeholders. Laitenberger and DeBaud (1997) split the tester into the module tester and the integration tester. A maintainer has a high interest in the source code and he or she is concerned if the code is easily understandable to allow future modification with minimal effort. Code can also be checked if it is compliant to coding standards and guidelines. This latter checking can be accomplished with modern tools. Laitenberger et al. (2001) recommended two perspectives for reading, which is the minimal set of viewpoints. They argued that there is some quantitative evidence that a two-person inspection team decreases inspection cost while maintaining its effectiveness (Bisant & Lyle, 1989); there is little difference in the inspection effectiveness of two- and four-person inspections (both are significantly better than one-person inspection) (Porter et al., 1997); and code in practice is inspected by a small team (Gilb & Graham, 1993).

A code analyst locates different functions in the code file, reads and understands them, and forms high-level abstractions. When reading source code, he or she can use any code reading techniques such as stepwise abstraction for structured code or abstraction-driven reading for object-oriented code, which are discussed in a later chapter. The reader then compares the high-level abstraction to the code specification and notes any deviation as a potential defect. The reader has a set of limited questions to answer, specifically designed for his or her reading perspective, based on the code documents and the understanding the reader achieved at this point. A sample reading scenario is shown in Panel 4-5: PBR – Code Reading Scenario for Code Analysts, which is adapted from Laitenberger et al. (2001).

PANEL 4-5: PBR – CODE READING SCENARIO FOR CODE ANALYSTS

Introduction: Assume the code analyst reading perspective, who has to ensure the right functionalities are implemented in code.

Instructions: Locate the functions implemented in the code. Use the stepwise abstraction reading technique if it is a structured code; use the abstraction-driven and use-case-driven reading techniques if it is object-oriented code. Start with the least-dependent code and read bottom-up to form a high-level abstraction of the coded function. For each function, check if the abstraction you derived matches the specification; if there is a deviation, decide if it is a defect and log your findings.

Questions: While following the instruction above, answer questions:

1. Does the operation implemented in code match the one described in the specification?

2. Is there any operation described in the specification, but not implemented in the code?

3. Are data (constants, variables, etc) and their type used correctly?

4. Is the calculation performed correctly?

5. Is usage of the interface between different modules semantically correct?

A code tester identifies different functions implemented in the code and develops and runs test cases on them to ensure their correctness. The reader then mentally simulates the execution of each function guided by test cases and compares the outcome with specifications. Any deviation shall be noted as a potential defect. If test cases have been developed during design reading, those test cases can be reused here. The reader also has a set of limited questions to answer, specifically designed for this tester reading perspective. Those questions are intended to focus the reader's attention. A sample tester reading scenario is shown in Panel 4-6: PBR – Code Reading Scenario for Code Testers, which is adapted from Laitenberger et al. (2001).

PANEL 4-6: PBR – CODE READING SCENARIO FOR CODE TESTERS

Introduction: Assume the tester reading perspective, which has to ensure the functionalities implemented in code are correct.

Instructions: Locate the functions implemented in code. Determine the dependencies among these functions and build a call graph from them. Start with the nodes with the least dependencies and traverse the call graph backward, and develop or reuse test cases that allow you to mentally simulate the execution of the function implemented by the node to cover all branches and loops. For each simulated execution, compare the outcome with that in specification. If there is a discrepancy, decide if it is a defect and log your findings.

Questions: While following the instruction above, answer questions:

1. Do you have all required information to identify a test case?

2. Are branch conditions implemented correctly?

3. Can you generate test cases for all branches and loops? Can you traverse all branches by some use cases? Does the outcome of each test case match the specification?

4. Is memory allocated and deallocated properly?

5. Can you traverse the call graph?

As we move down from design to implementation, the details are revealed gradually. In this code reading scenario, we are able to ask concrete questions, e.g., on the memory usage and branch implementations and coverage. This reading scenario is meant for module or unit testers as well as module integration testers.

4.3.4.2   Empirical Experiences

Laitenberger et al. (2001) ran a quasi-experiment and two replicates on professional software developers to compare the performances of perspective-based reading and checklist-based reading of C programming files. It is a quasi-experiment, since they piggybacked experiments on their industrial training opportunities and they didn't have control over all experimental conditions. They used two reading perspectives, analyst and tester. Defects were pooled through defect collection meetings and defects gain or loss effects in meetings were almost non-existing, thus ignored. Meta-analysis was conducted on the three experiments whenever possible. The researchers reported that perspective-based code reading had a slightly higher team defect detection effectiveness than checklist-based reading. The difference was statistically significant. Although individual using perspectives seems to require more effort (time) to detect a defect, the extra effort seems to be justified on the team level, since the team has a better cost per defect. The difference was significant on the team level using meta-analysis. The meeting cost of perspective-based reading was lower. Conjectured reasons include an increased understanding enabled by perspectives. When all costs (individual reading and defect collection meeting) were considered, perspective-based reading had a lower cost per defect and less variability than checklist-based reading.

4.3.5   Perspective-Based Usability Reading

Usability is concerned with how easy it is for a user to perform a desired task and what supports the system provides to the user to accomplish the task. It comprises the following aspects: learning system features, using the system efficiently, minimizing the impact of errors, adapting the system to user needs, and increasing user confidence and satisfaction (Bass et al., 2013). Experiences indicate that focusing on usability is the easiest and cheapest way to improve the user's perceived system quality. In this section we discuss how the ideas of perspective-based reading can be applied to inspect usability of software applications.

4.3.5.1   Reading Scenarios for Usability

Usability problems can be detected with usability inspection or usability testing. In usability testing, usability problems are found through the observation of and interaction with users while they use or comment on the user interface. In usability inspection, problems are found through the expertise of the inspectors and the inspection techniques they employ. The latter costs much less than the former, and heuristic evaluation, cognitive walkthrough, and guidelines and checklists are common inspection techniques in practice. However, their effectiveness (percent of problems detected) is rather low, particularly for non-experts (Zhang et al., 1999).

To improve the problem of detection effectiveness, Zhang et al. (1999) proposed a perspective-based usability inspection method known as use-based reading. They divided the large variety of usability issues along different perspectives (novice use, expert use, and error handling) and held multiple inspection sessions, each focusing on one particular perspective. Each perspective provides the inspector a point of view, a list of questions to check, which represents typical usability issues related to the perspective, and a specific procedure to perform the inspection. Just as perspective-based reading of other software artifacts, the focused attention, and well-defined procedure improve the inspector's problem detection performance related to the given perspective, and the combination of multiple orthogonal perspectives provides a better coverage of the usability spectrum and uncovers more usability issues.

People use computers to accomplish a task, and the usability or lack of it is exhibited during the human-computer interaction (HCI), which can be abstracted as the repetition of the following sequence of steps: form the goal, form the intention, identify the action, execute the action, perceive the system response, interpret the results, understand the outcome, and deal with errors if any. This sequence of steps can be summarized as execution and evaluation, with possible error correction. Therefore, usability issues are categorized as the gulf of execution (the mismatch between the user's intention and the computer action) and the gulf of evaluation (the mismatch between the user's expectation and system's representation) (Zhang et al., 1999). This simplistic HCI model guides the development of reading perspectives.

Usability perspectives are scenarios of HCI, and different perspectives emphasize different stages in the HCI model or different aspects of the same stage. Based on whether the user knows how to achieve a certain goal and whether the user executes the action correctly, Zhang et al. identified three perspectives: novice use, expert use, and error handling.

For the novice use perspective, the user does not have a deep knowledge regarding how to use the system to achieve his or her goal. Thus the usability goal is for the novice users with minimum knowledge to accomplish basic tasks. For the expert use perspective, the user knows how to use the system but wants to accomplish the task efficiently or easily or to achieve other higher goals. Thus the usability goal is for the expert users to complete tasks efficiently and easily, customize the system to their desire, and use advanced functions or features for improved productivity. For the error handling perspective, the user has a problem with the effect of the previous action and needs to correct the problem. Thus the usability goal is to minimize the chance to commit an error (error prevention), help the user to understand the situation once errors happen, allow the user recover from errors (error recovery), and deal with system failure appropriately. Questions in reading scenarios help the reader decide if the usability goals can be met or not and report usability gaps if not.

Panel 4-7: PBR – Expert Use Reading Scenarios shows the expert use reading scenarios adapted from Zhang et al. (1999). The scenarios are designed specifically for a web-based data collection form application.

Although the exact questions depend on the application being assessed, the intention is similar. The above expert use reading scenario aims at checking the user interface for its efficiency, flexibility, and consistency in supporting the user tasks, as well as the appropriateness of its visual appearance and organization, which supports the usability goal of the expert use discussed above.

While the perspective-based usability inspection of Zhang et al. partitions reading scenarios from the use point of view (novice, expert, and error handling), there are alternative ways to partition reading scenarios. Conte et al. (2009) decomposed scenarios from design perspectives. They identified conceptual, presentation, and navigation design perspectives for web applications that are used to guide the interpretation of commonly used heuristics. Combinations of the heuristics and design perspectives have yielded a set of specific reading guidance. The researchers also developed and evaluated a tool to support their reading technique (Vaz et al., 2013). Interested readers can refer to their papers for details.

PANEL 4-7: PBR – EXPERT USE READING SCENARIOS

Introduction: Assume you are an expert user. Your goal is to fill out the web form and submit it, which can be decomposed into multiple sub-goals in order. For each sub-goal, go through the following stages and check the questions. If your answer to a question is no, raise a usability issue.

Reading Instruction 1: Scan through instruction, objects, and actions in the user interface.

Question set 1:

1. Is the text easy to read?

2. Is the information organized such that the most important information can be read first?

3. Are the more frequently selected items arranged on top in the list control?

4. Is redundant information avoided or minimized?

Reading Instruction 2: Execute the actions for achieving the sub-goal, using shortcuts whenever available. For each action, check the following questions.

Question set 2:

1. Are common shortcuts available, e.g., to allow user to step to the next text field via keyboard?

2. Are possible default values provided?

3. Does the system compute and remember information for the user whenever possible?

4. Can the user make a selection by clicking on a larger area associated with the object to be selected?

5. Are unproductive activities avoided or minimized, e.g., navigation, mouse movement, hand movement, eye movement, etc.?

6. Are stressful actions avoided or minimized, e.g., clicking mouse multiple times in a short period of time, clicking on a small object to make a selection, etc.?

7. Is the text easy to read?

Reading Instruction 3: Wait for system to respond, if necessary.

Question set 3:

1. Does each user action immediately generate perceivable results in the user interface?

General question: In addition to the specific questions in Question set 3, consider this high-level question: Can the web form be redesigned to reduce the user's unproductive activities?

4.3.5.2   Empirical Experiences

Zhang et al. used professionals (programmers, domain experts, technique researchers, and cognitive researchers) as subjects and compared the use-based reading and the heuristic evaluation in inspecting the usability of a web-based data collection form. Heuristic evaluation is a popular inspection technique in practice. It gives the same general responsibility and provides a list of usability issues to participants, which is similar to ad hoc reading discussed earlier. The heuristics used include: speak the users' language, remain consistency, minimize the users' memory load and fatigue, flexibility and efficiency of use, use visually functional design, design for easy navigation, conduct validation checks, facilitate data entry, and provide sufficient guidance. They reported that perspective-based usability inspection found not only more issues related to their assigned perspectives but also more overall problems. When issues from three perspective readings were aggregated, the use-based reading uncovered about 30% more problems. Assigning inspectors more specific, focused responsibilities leads to improved performance, and combining multiple perspective focused inspections is a good strategy for creating high usability user interfaces.

4.3.6   Why Does Perspective-Based Reading Work?

As discussed earlier, perspective-based reading has been adapted and applied to software artifacts such as requirements specification, design description and graphical models and diagrams, source code and specifications, and user interface usability. Some experiments have been replicated internally and externally. Researchers reported both positive and negative experiences, and sometimes contradicting findings. To navigate through the collection of replicated experiments and associated findings, Ciolkowski (2009) performed a meta-analysis, which proved to be challenging, given the fact that the data were reported differently and important information was sometimes missing. Nevertheless, the author concluded that for requirements documents, perspective-based reading was significantly more effective than ad hoc reading; for design and code documents, perspective-based reading was significantly more effective than checklist-based reading, but for requirements documents, it was less effective.

This section discusses a cognitive analysis that sheds light on what is going on during perspective-based reading and how people's experiences play a role during reading. We also discuss a simple analytical model that provides indicative information when perspective-based reading can outperform other reading techniques.

4.3.6.1   Cognitive Analysis of Perspective-Based Reading

The cognitive analysis from cognitive science has been applied to the understanding of software inspection meetings. Letovsky et al. (1987) videotaped a representative code inspection meeting at IBM and analyzed it in detail. Their observational results suggested that participants were attempting to achieve three goals (clarity, correctness, and consistency) by executing three corresponding behaviors (design reconstruction, mental simulation, and document cross-checking). These categories accounted for 89% of the duration of the session. Robbins and Carver (2009) have applied a similar protocol analysis to perspective-based reading of requirements. Unlike the defect collection meeting, individual's reading of the software document typically happens quietly. To work around that, readers were requested to think aloud, i.e., they just spoke whatever in their mind at the moment during their reading. To facilitate the analysis, verbal reports during reading were coded and categorized.

Perspective-based reading is a complex problem-solving task that is focused on the problem of detecting defects in documents. A simplistic view of the task is illustrated in Figure 4-3, where the sensory input of the documents, including the requirements document, reading scenario description, and worksheet to log defects, goes through the sensory memory that feeds to the short-term memory. An individual's knowledge on the application domain, software and programming experience, the general knowledge on reading techniques, as well as the knowledge on the reading document newly acquired during reading are stored in the long-term memory, which is retrieved and sent to the short-term memory. All problem-solving tasks are performed in the short-term memory and the outcome is formed as a response.

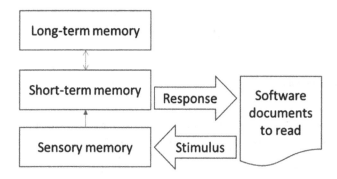

Figure 4-3. *Basic memory model in software reading (Adapted from Robbins & Carver [2009]).*

Verbal reports during reading were audio-recorded. Words or rephrases spoken by readers were captured and sometimes cross-checked with the defect worksheet, which were coded according to the model above:

- Any mentioning of reading of the requirements document, scenario description, and worksheet was coded as stimulus inputs with their respective codes.

- Any mentioning or recalling of previous knowledge or facts on the requirements document, training, perspective reading technique, domain knowledge, software, or programming knowledge was coded as retrievals from long-term memory using their respective codes.

- Any mentioning of combining existing knowledge into a single fact or making assumption on the document was coded as manipulation in short-term memory with their respective codes.

- Any mentioning or action of writing on the worksheet or logging defect was coded as response output with their respective codes.

The researchers ran the experiment using graduate and upper-level undergraduate students as subjects. The requirements document was about a web-based conference paper submission and review system. Only user and tester perspectives were used. The codes were analyzed using a frequency-based method. The authors were able to confirm:

- Most defect identifications were preceded by combining knowledge actions, which corresponds to the "defect trigger."

- The type of defects found by readers was related to the assigned reading perspectives, user, or tester. That is, the perspectives actually lead to detection of perspective-related defects.

- Perspective specific experience significantly affected the perspective-based reading process.

The protocol analysis provides a robust approach to understanding the cognitive mechanisms supporting perspective-based reading. It has a potential to reconcile all seemingly contradictory observations on the reading technique.

4.3.6.2   An Analytical Model

We can use a simple model to analyze when perspective-based reading outperforms other reading techniques such as checklist-based reading. Assume we have two reading scenarios A and B. Referring to Figure 4-4, Scenario A is designed to uncover defects in oval A, and similarly Scenario B is designed to uncover defects in oval B. In terms of defect detection, two reading scenarios have an overlap, which is the common area of ovals A and B. There are A number of defects that are covered by Scenario A, but not B, B number of defects that are covered by Scenario B, but not A, and C number of defects that are covered by both Scenarios A and B. We denote those regions also as A, B, and C. To put it another way, regions A and C are covered by Scenario A and regions B and C are covered by Scenario B. There are A+B+C total number of defects. Further assume there are no other defects and both perspective-based and checklist-based readings are perfect and they can potentially detect all defects existing in the document.

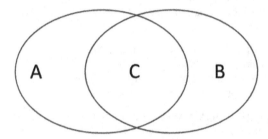

Figure 4-4. *Defects distribution*

We adopt a probabilistic view on defect detection. With Scenario A, defects that Scenario A is targeting will be detected with probability p_A, and other defects that Scenario A is not targeting will be detected with probability q_A. A reasonable assumption is that $p_A > q_A$. Similarly with Scenario B, we have probabilities p_B and q_B. To simplify the matter, we assume $p_A = p_B = p$ and $q_A = q_B = q$.

Assume that defect detections using Scenarios A and B are independent. When pooling defects together via, e.g., a defect collection meeting, there is no meeting gain or loss, which is a reasonable assumption according to Porter et al. (1995) and many others (e.g., Laitenberger et al. [2001]). Also assume that whether individual defects will be detected is independent of each other. A defect in region A will be missed if and only if both Scenarios A and B miss it, the probability of which is $(1-p)(1-q)$. Similarly, a defect in region B will be missed with the same probability $(1-p)(1-q)$. A defect in region C will be missed with probability $(1-p)^2$, however. Therefore, perspective-based reading using Scenarios A and B by a two-reader team will report, on average, D_{pbr} number of defects, as show below:

$$D_{pbr} = A \cdot \left[1-(1-p)(1-q)\right] + B \cdot \left[1-(1-p)(1-q)\right] + C$$
$$\cdot \left[1-(1-p)^2\right]$$

The first term on the right-hand side of the equation is the number of defects uncovered from region A, the second term is the number of defects uncovered from region B, and the last term is the number of defects uncovered from region C, by Scenarios A and/or B. With simple algebraic operations, this equation can be turned into

$$D_{pbr} = (A+B) \cdot (p+q-pq) + C \cdot (2p-p^2)$$

For checklist-based reading, let's assume there are two independent readers with the same defect detection probability s. It is logical to assume p>s>q. Otherwise there is no point to develop and utilize perspective-based reading. The checklist covers all potential defects. Therefore checklist-based reading from two readers will report, on average, D_{cbr} number of defects:

$$D_{cbr} = (A+B+C) \cdot \left(1-(1-s)^2\right)$$

With simplification, this amounts to

$$D_{cbr} = (A+B+C) \cdot (2s-s)^2$$

We shall find the difference D_{pbr}-D_{cbr}:

$$\Delta = D_{pbr} - D_{cbr} = (A+B) \cdot (p+q-pq-2s-s)^2 +$$
$$C \cdot (2p-p^2-2s+s^2)$$

Since $2p-p^2$ is an increasing function for p within 0 and 1 and p>s, the second term on the right-hand side is always positive. We shall seek one sufficient condition so that perspective-based reading outperforms checklist-based reading, which is

$$p+q-pq-2s+s^2 \geq 0$$

This is not a necessary condition, since the second term on the right-hand side (i.e. the term involving C) is always positive if p>s, which may offset the first (negative) term (i.e., the term involving A+B) and still make perspective-based reading better.
The sufficient condition can be re-rendered, following the steps below:

$$p-pq-s+sq \geq s-q-s^2+sq$$
$$(p-s)(1-q) \geq -(1-s)(s-q)$$
$$p-s \geq \frac{1-s}{1-q}(s-q)$$

This is the same equation as A28 in Laitenberger et al. [2001]. The difference p-s can be considered as the gained efficiency of defect detection for defects covered by reading scenario, and s-q the lost efficiency for defects not covered by reading scenario. That is, when the gained and lost efficiencies satisfy the above relationship because of the scenario focusing, perspective-based reading can outperform checklist-based reading.

We shall note that $\frac{1-s}{1-q} < 1$ when s>q.

Let's use some real numbers to put it into quantitative basis. In Figure 4-5 we plot the relationship between p and q for s=0.4, 0.5, and 0.6. For those s values, the corresponding defect detection effectiveness defined in percentages are 64%, 75%, and 84%, respectively. For a given curve, when p is above the curve line, perspective-based reading will be more effective than checklist-based reading. The smaller q is, the more focused the reading is. The diagram also points the direction to how one can make perspective-based reading more effective. If we suppress the defect detection probability for the non-scenario-targeted defects, we have to increase the detection probability for the scenario-targeted defects and the quantitative relationship of loss and gain is related by the formula given earlier. If one completely misses the defects not targeted by the reading scenario (i.e., q=0), the detection effectiveness of the targeted defect p has to be at least $2s-s^2$ in order to be better than the baseline reading technique.

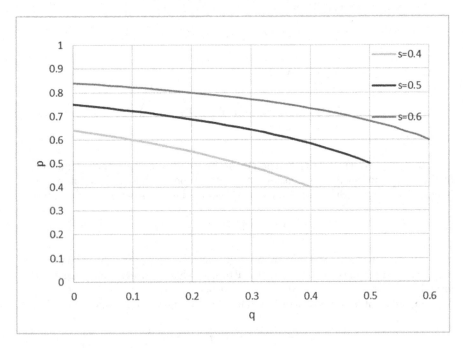

Figure 4-5. *The p-q phase diagram*

Contradicting experimental results can be understood within this theoretical framework.

1. We first point out that this simple relationship is obtained under the assumption that reading techniques, perspective-based reading, and any other techniques that perspective-based reading is compared to can uncover all defects. In reality, experimental conditions may not satisfy this assumption. We didn't see any analysis to confirm that all defects could be uncovered, in theory, using the investigated reading techniques.

2. In practice, we also find that some defects are easy to uncover, while others are not so. That is, each defect has a different probability to be detected. The analysis assumes a uniform detection probability in the defect groups (the perspective targeted or not targeted, or the entire defects).

3. When designing reading perspectives for their targeted defects, we purposely minimize the defects overlap, i.e., C region in the diagram. This turns out to be a very difficult objective to achieve. There is no discussion from experimental designers regarding how the defect overlapping region looked like in their experiment. The existence of a common region favors perspective-based reading, however (see the second term in D_{pbr}-D_{cbr}).

4. The defect detection probability, p, q, and s, strongly depends on an individual's experience and skill. In all published experiments, there was no explicit estimate of those probabilities. Hence, when perspective-based reading outperforms other reading techniques, we are not clear why and how we attribute its success; when it does not outperform, we don't know why it is so.

5. For future experiments, we suggest researchers collect or estimate those data so that the results can be analyzed quantitatively and the success can be properly attributed to.

Let's examine the common defects detected by two reading perspectives. This is not the common region C in the diagram, as the defects not targeted by a reading scenario are detected at a probability q. In the two-person team, on average, the common defects reported by both team members are, respectively, for perspective-based reading and checklist-based reading:

$$D_{pbr}^c = (A+B) \cdot pq + C \cdot p^2$$
$$D_{cbr}^c = (A+B+C) \cdot s^2$$

With those two quantities, we can rewrite the difference as

$$\Delta = (A+B)\cdot(p+q-2s) + 2C\cdot(p-s) + \left(D_{cbr}^{c} - D_{pbr}^{c}\right)$$

In literature it was believed that the effectiveness of perspective-based reading was due to the reduction of overlapping defect detection (i.e. reduced value of D_{pbr}^{c}). We argue this is not necessarily the case. Suppose we have perfectly focused reading scenarios that do not detect any defects the scenarios are not targeting, i.e., q=0. In that case the overlapping defects detected by perspective-based reading is D_{pbr}^{c}=0 when C=0 or A+B>>C, and of course, to ensure Δ>0, p has to satisfy some condition, which would be p>2s-s². Now suppose for a given p and q, two reading techniques give the same performance, i.e., Δ=0. Now holding q constant, we improve the reading scenarios such that all targeted defects are detected with probability p=1. Δ increases as p increases and perspective-based reading outperforms checklist-based reading. Since we fix the value of q and improve the value of p, the overlapping defects detected by perspective-based reading D_{pbr}^{c} increases. In other words, the outperforming perspective-based reading has an increased number of defects detected by both reading scenarios. How the overlapping defects are detected by perspective-based reading is not the driving force if perspective-based reading outperforms the baseline reading technique. Rather it is the consequence of the change in detection capabilities for the defects targeted and not targeted by the perspectives. How the number of detected overlapping defects will change is determined by the relative changes of those detection capabilities.

4.4   Alternative Partitioning of Reading Responsibilities

We have discussed two scenario-based reading techniques, defect-based reading and perspective-based reading. While defect-based reading partitions scenarios based on defect classes, perspective-based reading decomposes scenarios based on stakeholders' perspectives to the documents under review. When a defect or perspective scenario is assigned to a reader, the portion or aspect of the document is assigned to the reader implicitly. There exist other alternatives that partition the reading responsibilities and coordinate reading activities, however.

4.4.1   Ad hoc Partition

A document under review usually has multiple parts. If a template is used to write the document, it might have different chapters and sections. For example, a requirements specification of an IT application may have chapters on web interface, billing, database, etc. Among all those parts, a group of reviewers can decide how to assign different portions to different people. Cheng and Jeffery (1996) called this self-set strategy. The document author or review coordinator can make the assignment as well, based on readers' interests and expertise. Once the document review responsibilities are divided among readers, each reader can use whatever reading techniques they may possess, e.g., ad hoc reading or checklist-based reading. This ad hoc assignment reduces the work overload to individual readers and provides a specific area of focus for them, compared to the case where the whole document is given to reviewers and the reviewers are simply asked to detect as many defects as they could.

4.4.2   Function Point-Based Partition

Cheng and Jeffery (1996) developed a set of scenarios, function point scenarios, for requirements reading based on function point analysis. Functional user requirements can be categorized into five types: inputs, outputs, inquiries, internal files, and external interfaces. Each of those types can be easily mapped to end-user business function, e.g., an input mapped to a data entry, an inquiry mapped to a user query. Function point analysis is frequently used to estimate the complexity and effort of the software. The authors, however, used the five functional types to dissect the software system into orthogonal areas, which provides the basis for reading scenario construction. Five function point scenarios are:

- *Overview*: This is an overall description of the entire system. The purpose of this reading scenario is to check the overall relevance, completeness, and correctness of a requirements specification.

- *File*: This combines the internal files and external interfaces functional types, given that they have similar characteristics with respect to the requirements review. This contains the attributes for the purpose of the application.

- *Input*: This is a process that requests the inputs from a user or another system. The input may come as screen input or batch input.

- *Output*: This is the opposite as the input and generates information for a user or another system, which can be in a form of report, or data transferred to other processes.

- *Inquiry*: A process that retrieves data as a response to an input from a user or a process, and outputs the data to a user or another system. Data update is not involved in this process.

Key issues covered by each function point analysis are constructed into domain-specific questions, which are augmented by available checklist items. Those questions are used directly in a scenario description, which also provides instruction to focus the reader on specific areas of the requirements document related to the scenario/functional type.

Cheng and Jeffery used senior undergraduate and graduate students with industrial experience as subjects. They compared the defect detection performances of self-set strategy and function point scenarios and reported that the self-set strategy group detected more defects. The difference was not statistically significant though. They further reported that there was no significant difference in defect types either. While the reading using the self-set strategy showed a dependency on the individual experience, the same dependence was not observed in the subjects using the function point scenarios. The researchers could not tell if function point scenario-based reading helped the inexperienced readers or inhibited the experienced readers.

65

4.5 Summary

We have discussed three scenario-based reading techniques, defect-based reading, perspective-based reading, and function-point-based reading. The first and last reading techniques have been applied to requirements specification documents. Perspective-based reading has been customized to requirements, design, code, and usability reading and inspection. Due to experimental variabilities and human nature, both positive and negative findings were reported. We discussed a cognitive analysis that shed light on what is going on during perspective-based reading and analyzed a simple model to suggest when perspective-based reading can outperform other reading techniques. Perspective-based reading started to see some industrial adoption (Lahtinen, 2011). Later chapters will discuss additional scenario-based reading techniques, e.g., traceability-based reading.

4.6 References

(Basili, 1996) V.R. Basili, S. Green, O. Laitenberger, F. Lanubile, F. Shull, S. Sorumgard, and M.V. Zelkowitz, The empirical investigation of perspective-based reading, Empirical Software Engineering, vol.1, no.2, pp.133-164, 1996.

(Bass, 2013) L. Bass, P. Clements, and R. Kazman, Software Architecture in Practice, 3rd ed., Addison-Wesley, 2013.

(Bisant, 1989) D. Bisant and J. Lyle, A two-person inspection method to improve programming productivity, IEEE Transactions on Software Engineering, vol.15, no.10, pp.1294-1304, 1989.

(Chen, 2002) T.Y Chen, P.L. Poon, S.F. Tang, T.H. Tse, and Y.T. Yu, Towards a problem-driven approach to perspective-based reading, Proceedings of the 7th IEEE International Symposium on High Assurance Systems Engineering, pp.221-229, 2002.

(Cheng, 1996) B. Cheng and R. Jeffery, Comparing inspection strategies for software requirement specifications, Proceedings of Australian Software Engineering Conference, pp.201-211, 1996.

(Ciolkowski, 1997) M. Ciolkowski, C. Differding, O. Laitenberger, and J. Munch, Empirical investigation of perspective-based reading: A replicated experiment, Technical Report No.13, International Software Engineering Research Network, 1997.

(Ciolkowski, 2003) M. Ciolkowski, O. Laitenberger, and S. Biffl, Software reviews, the state of the practice, IEEE Software, vol.20, no.6, pp.46-51, 2003.

(Ciolkowski, 2009) M. Ciolkowski, What do we know about perspective-based reading? An approach for quantitative aggregation in software engineering, 3rd International Symposium on Empirical Software Engineering and Measurement, pp.133-144, 2009.

(Conte, 2009) T. Conte, J. Massolar, E. Mendes, and G.H. Travassos, Web usability inspection technique based on design perspectives, IET Software, vol.3, no.2, pp.106-123, 2009.

(Fagan, 1976) M.E. Fagan, Design and code inspections to reduce errors in program development, IBM Systems Journal, vol.15, no.3, pp.182-211, 1976.

(Fowler, 1986) P.J. Fowler, In-process inspections of workproducts at AT&T, AT&T Technical Journal, vol.65, no.2, pp.102-112, 1986. Also in Software Inspection: An Industry Best Practice, D.A. Wheeler, B. Brykczynski, and R.N. Meeson Jr., IEEE Computer Society Press, 1996.

(Fusaro, 1997) P. Fusaro, F. Lanubile, and G. Visagggio, A replicated experiment to assess requirements inspection techniques, Empirical Software Engineering, vol.2, no.1, pp.39-57, 1997.

(Gilb, 1993) T. Gilb and D. Graham, Software Inspection, Addison-Wesley, 1993.

(Graden, 1986) M.E. Graden, P.S. Horsley, and T.C. Pingel, The effects of software inspections on a major telecommunication project, AT&T Technical Journal, vol.65, no.3, pp.32-40, 1986. Also in Software Inspection: An Industry Best Practice, D.A. Wheeler, B. Brykczynski, and R.N. Meeson Jr., IEEE Computer Society Press, 1996.

(Hayes, 1999) W. Hayes, Research synthesis in software engineering: a case for meta-analysis, Proc. of the 6th International Software Metrics Symposium, pp.143-151, 1999.

(IEEE, 2008) IEEE, IEEE Standard for Software Reviews and Audits, IEEE Std 1028-2008.

(Lahtinen, 2011) J. Lahtinen, Application of the perspective-based reading technique in the nuclear I&C context, CORSICA work report, 2011.

(Laitenberger, 1997) O. Laitenberger and J.M. DeBaud, Perspective-based reading of code documents at Robert Bosch GmbH, Information and Software Technology, vol.39, no.11, pp.781-791, 1997.

(Laitenberger, 1999) O. Laitenberger and C. Atkinson, Generalizing perspective-based inspection to handle object-oriented development artifacts, Proceedings of the 21st International Conference on Software Engineering, pp.494-503, 1999.

(Laitenberger, 2000) O. Laitenberger, C. Atkinson, M. Schlich, K. El Emam, An experimental comparison of reading techniques for defect detection in UML design documents, Journal of Systems and Software, vol.53, no.2, pp.183-204, 2000.

(Laitenberger, 2001) O. Laitenberger, K. El Emam, and T.G. Harbich, An internally replicated quasi-experimental comparison of checklist and perspective-based reading of code documents, IEEE Transactions on Software Engineering, vol.27, no.5, pp.387-421, 2001.

(Letovsky, 1987) S. Letovsky, J. Pinto, R. Lampert, and E. Soloway, A cognitive analysis of a code inspection, in Empirical Studies of Programming, Chapter 15, G. Olson, S. Sheppard, E. Soloway, eds., pp.231-247, 1987. Also in Software Inspection: An Industry Best Practice, D.A. Wheeler, B. Brykczynski, and R.N. Meeson Jr., IEEE Computer Society Press, 1996.

(Maldonado, 2006) J.C. Maldonado, J. Carver, F. Shull, S. Fabbri, E. Doria, L. Martimiano, M. Mendonca, and V. Basili, Perspective-based reading: A replicated experiment focused on individual reviewer effectiveness, Empirical Software Engineering, vol.11, pp.119-142, 2006.

(Miller, 1998) J. Miller, M. Wood, and M. Roper, Further experiences with scenarios and checklists, Empirical Software Engineering, vol.3, no.1, pp.37-64, 1998.

(Parnas, 1985) D.L. Parnas and D.M. Weiss, Active design reviews: principles and practices, 8th International conference on Software Engineering, pp.215-222, 1985.

(Porter, 1994) A.A. Porter and L.G. Votta, An experiment to assess different defect detection methods for software requirements inspections, in Proceedings of the 16th International Conference on Software Engineering, pp.103-112, 1994.

(Porter, 1995) A.A. Porter, L.G. Votta, and V.R. Basili, Comparing detection methods for software requirements inspection: A replicated experiment, IEEE Transactions on Software Engineering, vol.21, no.6, pp.563-575, 1995.

(Porter, 1997) A.A. Porter, H.P. Siy, C.A. Toman, and L.G. Votta, An experiment to assess the cost-benefits of code inspection in large scale software development, IEEE Transactions on Software Engineering, vol.3, no.6, pp.329-346, 1997.

(Porter, 1998) A.A. Porter and L.G. Votta, Comparing detection methods for software requirements inspection: A replication using professional subjects, Empirical Software Engineering, vol.3, no.4, pp.355-379, 1998.

(Regnell, 2000) B. Regnell, P. Runeson, and T. Thelin, Are the perspective really different? – Further experimentation on scenario-based reading of requirements, Empirical Software Engineering, vol.5, no.4, pp.331-355, 2000.

(Robbins, 2009) B. Robbins and J. Carver, Cognitive factors in perspective-based reading (PBR): A protocol analysis study, 3rd International Symposium on Empirical Software Engineering and Measurement, pp.145-155, 2009.

(Sandahl, 1998) K. Sandahl, O. Blomkvist, J. Karlsson, C. Krysander, M. Lindvall, and N. Ohlsson, An extended replication of an experiment for assessing methods for software requirements inspection, Empirical Software Engineering, vol.3, no.4, pp.327-354, 1998.

(Sabaliauskaite, 2003) G. Sabaliauskaite, F. Matsukawa, S. Kusumoto, and K. Inoue, Further investigations of reading techniques for object-oriented design inspection, Information and Software Technology, vol.45, no.9, pp.571-585, 2003.

(Schulte, 2010) C. Schulte, T. Busjahn, T. Clear, J.H. Paterson, and A. Taherkhani, An introduction to program comprehension from computer science educators, Innovation and Technology in Computer Science Education Working Group Reports ITiCSE-WGR'10, pp.65-86, 2010.

(Shull, 2000) F. Shull, I. Rus, and V. Basili, How perspective-based reading can improve requirements inspections, IEEE Computer, vol.33, no,7, pp.73-79, 2000.

(Vaz, 2013) V.T. Vaz, T. Conte, G.H. Travassos, Empirical assessments of a tool to support web usability inspection, CLEI Electronic Journal vol.16 no.3, paper 6, 2013.

(Walia, 2009) G.S. Walia and J.C. Carver, A systematic literature review to identify and classify software requirement errors, Information and Software Technology, vol.51, pp.1087-1109, 2009.

(Zhang, 1999) Z. Zhang, V.R. Basili, B. Schneiderman, Perspective-based usability inspection: an empirical validation of efficacy, Empirical Software Engineering, vol.4, no.1, pp.43-69, 1999.

■ ■ ■

CHAPTER 5

Requirements Reading Techniques

The general reading techniques, ad hoc reading, checklist-based reading, defect-based reading, and perspective-based reading, have all been applied to inspect software requirements specifications. A detailed account of these techniques and their empirical experiences can be found in Chapters 3 and 4. Here we discuss additional reading techniques that are applicable specifically to requirements specifications. We also discuss what factors impact the effectiveness of requirements reading, which can be used to guide reading team selection and training.

5.1 Critical Roles of Requirements in Software Development

A requirements specification is an important document generated in the early stages of a software development project. It defines the functionality, scope, and constraints of the software system. It can also serve as a basis for contract negotiations or communication between the software development organization and end users.

The importance of the requirements specification cannot be emphasized enough. If the development is based on an incomplete and incorrect requirements specification, then the finished software product will not fulfill users' needs. Defects in a vague or ambiguous specification can be propagated down to subsequent development phases such as design and/or coding. Designers or developers would potentially still be able to catch these problems, but it will be at the expense of schedule delays, which can be costly. Even worse, if the defects remain undetected and a faulty software product is delivered to users, the users' working environment could be damaged. So it is paramount to read, detect, and correct requirements issues early in the development process.

© Yang-Ming Zhu 2016
Y.-M. Zhu, *Software Reading Techniques*, DOI 10.1007/978-1-4842-2346-8_5

5.2   A Combined Reading Technique for Requirements

The number and types of defects each reading technique can detect vary from one technique to another. A combined-reading (CR) technique is intended to take advantage of the strengths of individual reading techniques while compensating for their weaknesses.

5.2.1   Motivations for a Combined Reading

Checklist-based reading (CBR), defect-based reading (DBR), and perspective-based reading (PBR) techniques have all been applied to software requirements specifications. Maldonado et al. (2006) reported that PBR and CBR are complementary to each other for reading some requirements specifications. Alshazly et al. (2014) compared the three reading techniques and reported that, in terms of total number of defects detected, PBR > DBR > CBR ("> " means "is better than"); in terms of ambiguous and omission defect detection capability, PBR > DBR > CBR; in terms of inconsistent defect detection capability, PBR > DBR ≈ CBR ("≈" means "roughly the same as"); in terms of incorrect defect detection capability, DBR > CBR > PBR; and in terms of superfluous defect detection capability, CBR = DBR > PBR. Each reading technique has its own strength and weakness.

Thus it is difficult to detect most or all defects using a single reading technique alone. An apparent solution is to combine multiple reading techniques, which exploits the advantages of each reading technique and avoids its limitations at the same time.

5.2.2   The Combined-Reading Technique

A software requirements specification document has multiple constituent parts. For example, IEEE STD 830-1998 has a recommended structure for a software requirements specification (this recommendation has been superseded by ISO/IEC/IEEE 29148:2011). Not all classes of defects could occur in all parts of the document, and there is only a limited number of defect classes that could appear in a given part. The main idea behind CR is to examine every constituent parts of the software requirements specification in detail. For software organizations, the historical defect patterns and root causes can be analyzed to determine what classes of defects can occur in what parts of the document and how the defects are introduced. After that, specific questions can be developed for each part of the document to cover different types of defects from the perspectives of different stakeholders, taking into account defect history and the purpose of the individual parts of the requirements specification.

The influences of CBR, DBR, and PBR are apparent. Combined reading is based on defect class analysis, and specific questions are designed for it (DBR). The questions are designed to cover the defects from the perspectives of different stakeholders (PBR). The guidance is constructed as a list of yes/no questions (CBR).

An excerpt of the reading guidance is shown in Table 5-1, where checked items are the areas of concern, defect types are typical types of defects the organization may have, defect sources list the main and sub-error sources, and the checklist items are the questions for the reader to answer throughout the course of reading.

Table 5-1. *An Excerpt Guidance of the Combined Reading Technique (adapted from Alshazly et al. [2014])*

Q	Checked item	Defect type	Defect source		Checklist item
			Main	Sub	
1	External interfaces	Omission	Process	Analysis	Have all inputs and outputs of the system been described in detail?
2	User interfaces	Omission	People	Concentration	Have all interfaces between the software product and its users been specified?
3	Constraints	Omission	Process	Analysis	Do all significant consumers have scarce resources, such as memory, network bandwidth, processor capacity, etc. identified? Has the anticipated consumption of resources been specified?
4	Use-case name and number	Ambiguous	People	Concentration	Does the use-case name reflect its goal?
5		Inconsistent	Documentation	Organization	Are the requirements arranged numerically according to the logical order of occurrence and in order to prevent confusion between the requirements?
6		Inconsistent	Process	Traceability	Is there a conflict between the functional requirements names and the relevant use-cases names?
...					
68	Non-functional requirements	Omission	Process	Elicitation	Are the necessary non-functional requirements specified, including reliability, availability, security, maintainability, and portability?
69	General questions	Inconsistent	Documentation	Documentation standards	Did the author of the document use numbering levels to identify sections of the document and the functional requirements?

The CR technique guides the reader through what is being inspected and provides instruction on how the inspection should be conducted. The required training is minimal and a novice reader can benefit from it. As the empirical evidence shows, it is more effective than CBR, DBR, and PBR.

An apparent limitation of the CR technique is that the list of questions is relatively large (69 questions in total). It could be overwhelming to a single reader and would be more manageable if the questions were divided among multiple readers. The other drawback is, just like the checklist, it is effective for known defects and defect types but might not be so for defects not previously seen.

5.2.3   Empirical Experiences

Alshazly et al. (2014) applied the CR technique to four requirements specification documents and compared its defect detection effectiveness with those of CBR, DBR, and PBR in case studies. In terms of the total number of defects detected, CR > PBR > DBR > CBR; in terms of ambiguous defect detection capability, CR > CBR > DBR > PBR; in terms of inconsistent defect detection capability, CR > PBR > DBR ≈ CBR; in terms of incorrect defect detection capability, CR > DBR ≈ CBR > PBR; in terms of omission defect detection capability, CR > PBR > DBR > CBR; in terms of superfluous defect detection capability, CR > CBR ≈ DBR ≈ PBR; and in terms of non-conforming to standard defect detection capability, CR ≈ CBR ≈ DBR ≈ PBR. These findings have not been confirmed by independently replicated experiments yet.

5.3   Test-Case Driven Reading for Requirements

Most of the time when we read requirements, we detect and remove defects for a full-fledged project to avoid propagating issues down to subsequent development phases. The requirements document is typically inspected by multiple stakeholders. There are other situations in which we inspect the requirements to ensure that we have good enough requirements to support decision making during planning and before the project is kicked off (pre-project), e.g., what requirements to select for realization and cost estimation. Companies operating in a market-driven environment typically have a large amount of requirements coming from different sources with different levels of quality. With limited resources, they want to inspect the requirements in a lean manner and amortize the effort across different development phases, since they have many more pre-project requirements than their development organization can handle. Gorschek and Fogelstrom (2005) and Fogelstrom and Gorschek (2007) developed a test-case-driven requirements reading to satisfy the above needs. They proposed an inspection process in which the test-case-driven reading is embedded. Here we focus on the reading technique.

5.3.1   Test-Case-Driven Reading Technique

The goal of the test-case-driven reading technique is to enable the software development organization to inspect the requirements effectively with minimal cost. It utilizes the test-cases as a tool for inspection and involves real testers at an early stage of the pre-project decision making. The test-cases developed during reading can be used in latter development phases, and thus the cost and time demand in the early requirement phase is spread along the project phases.

The tester ensures the testability, completeness, and non-conflicting aspects of those requirements. If the tester can create test-cases based on a requirement, then the requirement is considered testable. Since the tester is an expert in the use of the system, any missing or incomplete functionality can be easily detected. This provides another angle for the tester to examine the system, from the perspective of the end-user. When the tester goes through the set of requirements thoroughly by creating test-cases along the way, any conflicting and inconsistent requirements can be caught.

We shall contrast test-case-driven reading with perspective-based reading to further understand the test-case-driven reading technique:

- To support PBR, reading scenarios, including the tester's reading scenario, must be developed and maintained from different stakeholders' perspectives. In test-case-driven reading, no reading scenario is required since the real testers are employed.

- In the tester's PBR, individuals such as requirements engineers or developers—not necessarily the real testers—are employed to simulate the tester's perspective. Thus education, training, and practice will be required for these readers. In test-case-driven reading, the experienced testers are doing the reading, which not only represents the tester's perspective better than the simulated one, but also alleviates the education and training costs. This might also utilize resources better, since typically, the testers could have a light workload during the requirements definition phase if there are no other active projects.

- In the tester's PBR, the reader develops test cases. Since these test cases are developed by non-testers, it is always in question whether these test cases can be reused in a later phase. In test-case-driven reading, the tester's competence and efforts are exploited to develop test-cases, which serves the inspection for now, and could also be reused in later development and testing phases. The test-cases can be used to augment the requirements so that developers understand the requirements better, which reduces the chance of misinterpreting the requirements.

- Perspective-based reading typically takes advantages of the perspectives of multiple stakeholders, with each reader representing one perspective. However, test-case-driven reading utilizes one tester who brings two perspective: tester and end-user. The tester's perspective is an obvious one. The tester is familiar with the real usage of the system. He or she is thus a system functionality expert and an expert at reading and interpreting the requirements.

5.3.2 Empirical Experiences

Gorschek and Fogelstrom (2005) conducted a pilot study and concluded that the benefit of test-case-driven requirements reading was substantial based on the subjective feedback from people who were involved. Product managers felt the inspected and reworked requirements were of high quality, offered better support for decision making, prevented unviable requirements from passing down to the next step, and improved the product manager's requirements specification skills. The testers felt it enabled them to create a realistic test plan early. However, they also reported that non-functional requirements were hard to inspect due to potential conflicts among different quality attributes.

In a follow-up study, Fogelstrom and Gorschek (2007) compared test-case-driven requirements reading to CBR, using software engineering graduate students as subjects. They reported that CBR found a high amount of false positive defects, but fewer major defects. Conflicting requirements, missing requirements, and missing or wrong information in requirements are considered major. When only major defects were considered, test-case-driven reading is 44% to 55% more effective than CBR, where the effectiveness is defined as the percentage of major defects uncovered among the total major defects. When efficiency is concerned (number of major defects uncovered per hour), the result is not conclusive. In one case, test-case-driven reading is more efficient, and in the other case, CBR is more efficient, but the difference is not significant in both cases.

5.4 Individual Factors Impacting Requirements Reading Efficiency

Researchers have reported that individual defect detection performance can vary by a factor of 10 in terms of defects found per unit time (Hatton, 2008). This wide variation in the defect detection effectiveness (total number of defects or the percentage of defects detected) is also reported, even when readers are using the same technique and same process on the same artifact. For example, Basili et al. (1996) reported that the effectiveness of individual readers ranged from 10% to 90% when applying PBR on requirements specifications. Similar variation exhibits at the team level as well (Schneider et al., 1992). We often see different, sometimes contradicting, empirical findings in replicated experiments (Hayes, 1999; Ciolkowski, 2009). People's backgrounds and experiences play a significant role during software reading and analysis. It is thus prudent to study what factors impact the effectiveness of requirements reading.

Miller and Yin (2004) studied a characteristic of readers not related to software engineering expertise, the Myers-Briggs personality type. Miller and Yin reported that personality type was not a good predictor of the individual effectiveness of requirements reading. However, a team formed by people of different personalities with diverse information processing strategies maximizes the number of different defects detected.

Biffl and Halling (2002) studied the characteristics directly related to software engineering expertise, development skills, quality assurance experience, and performance on a pre-test with a mini-inspection. Biffl and Halling concluded that only readers' performance on a pre-test of mini-inspection, not their development and quality assurance capability and experience, was considerably correlated to reading performance. Two other software engineering characteristics, IT experience and data-flow diagram experience, were investigated by Hungerford et al. (2004) with experienced software developers. Although the researchers did not find that these characteristics affect reading performance, they reported that the ability to rapidly switch between diagrams impacted the reading performance.

Carver et al. (2008) studied the impact of educational background (field of study), education degree, and requirements writing experience on requirements defect detection effectiveness using professionals as subjects. The researchers reported that readers with an education background not related to computing such as engineering, math, science, business, or the arts, were significantly more effective in detecting omission and inconsistency defects. Upon further analysis, readers with computer science or software engineering background were the least effective. Readers with requirements writing experience were significantly more effective than those without, regardless of whether the experience was gained through industry practice or classroom learning. Their effectiveness was not related to particular defect categories. Education degree was not found to be significantly related to defect detection performance. The experiment of Carver et al. was replicated by Albayrak and Carver (2014) with industry practitioners in a different country. The original findings were confirmed in the replicated study.

The reason people with computing-related education backgrounds have poor defect detection effectiveness is not well understood. One possible reason is that people with computing backgrounds tend to think in terms of design and coding immediately upon reading requirements. Meanwhile, people with non-computing backgrounds may approach requirements as a user, rather than designer or implementer. Another possible explanation might be that precise writing was part of training in non-computing fields.

The research findings discussed earlier have interesting implications to software inspection practice in industry. When selecting people to inspect software artifacts, it is a wise decision to select people with different education backgrounds, particularly those with non-computing-related disciplines. If defect collection meetings will be held, people with different personality types should be chosen as well. When inspecting software requirements specification documents, it is good to include people with requirements writing experience.

5.5 Summary

Software requirements specifications play a critical role during the software development process and it is important to get them right as early as possible. Ad hoc reading and CBR are mostly used in practice. Scenario-based reading, DBR, and PBR in particular, have been applied to requirements reading with reported success. This chapter discusses a few newly proposed reading techniques: CR, which combines the benefits of the CBR, DBR, and PBR techniques, and test-case-driven reading, which is applicable to organizations with limited resources and can provide good-enough requirements for project decision making early in the software development lifecycle. It is known that individuals with different backgrounds exhibit a varying performance in software reading. Factors that impact requirements reading performance are discussed, which can be utilized when assembling and training a requirements inspection team.

5.6 References

(Albayrak, 2014) O. Albayrak and J.C. Carver, Investigation of individual factors impacting the effectiveness of requirements inspections: a replicated experiment, Empirical Software Engineering, vol.19, pp.241-266, 2014.

(Alshazly, 2014) A.A. Alshazly, A.M. Elfatatry, and M.S. Abougabal, Detecting defects in software requirements specification, Alexandria Engineering Journal, vol.53, pp.513-527, 2014.

(Basili, 1996) V.R. Basili, S. Green, O. Laitenberger, F. Lanubile, F. Shull, S. Sorumgard, and M.V. Zelkowitz, The empirical investigation of perspective-based reading, Empirical Software Engineering, vol.1, no.2, pp.133-164, 1996.

(Biffl, 2002) S. Biffl and M. Halling, Investigating the influence of inspector capability factors with four inspection techniques on inspection performance, Proceedings of 8th IEEE Symposium on Software Metrics, pp.107-117, 2002.

(Carver, 2008) J.C. Carver, N. Nagappan, and A. Page, The impact of educational background on the effectiveness of requirements inspections: an empirical study, IEEE Transactions on Software Engineering, vol.34, no.6, pp.800-812, 2008.

(Ciolkowski, 2009) M. Ciolkowski, What do we know about perspective-based reading? An approach for quantitative aggregation in software engineering, 3rd International Symposium on Empirical Software Engineering and Measurement, pp.133-144, 2009.

(Fogelstrom, 2007) N.D. Fogelstrom and T. Gorschek, Test-case driven versus checklist-based inspections of software requirements – An experimental evaluation, Workshop emEngenharia de Requisitos, pp.116-126, 2007.

(Gorschek, 2005) T. Gorschek and N.D. Fogelstrom, Test-case driven inspections of pre-project requirements – Process proposal and industry experience report, Proceedings of the Requirements Engineering Decision Support Workshop held in conjunction with the 13th IEEE International Conference on Requirements Engineering, 2005.

(Hatton, 2008) L. Hatton, Testing the value of checklists in code inspections, IEEE Software, vol.25, no.4, pp.82-88, 2008.

(Hayes, 1999) W. Hayes, Research synthesis in software engineering: a case for meta-analysis, Proc. of the 6th International Software Metrics Symposium, pp.143-151, 1999.

(Hungerford, 2004) B.C. Hungerford, A.R. Hevner, and R.W. Collins, Reviewing software diagrams: A cognitive study, IEEE Transactions on Software Engineering, vol.30, no.2, pp.82-96, 2004.

(Maldonado, 2006) J.C. Maldonado, J. Carver, F. Shull, S. Fabbri, E. Doria, L. Martimiano, M. Mendonca, and V. Basili, Perspective-based reading: A replicated experiment focused on individual reviewer effectiveness, Empirical Software Engineering, vol.11, pp.119-142, 2006.

(Miller, 2004) J. Miller and Z. Yin, A cognitive-based mechanism for constructing software inspection teams, IEEE Transactions on Software Engineering, vol.30, no.11, pp.811-825, 2004.

(Schneider, 1992) G.M. Schneider, J. Martin, and W.T. Tsai, An experimental study of fault detection in user requirements documents, ACM Transactions on Software Engineering and Methodology, vol.1, no.2, pp.188-204, 1992.

CHAPTER 6

■ ■ ■

Design Reading Techniques

The general reading techniques discussed in Chapters 3 and 4, ad hoc reading, checklist-based reading, and perspective-based reading, have all been applied to inspect design documents. This chapter discusses a few more reading techniques applicable specifically to design artifacts, namely usage-based reading, traceability-based reading, and scope-based reading.

6.1   Introduction

In a software development process, the development of software architecture and design is between requirements engineering and code implementation. Thus software design needs to satisfy a requirements specification and provide guidance to subsequent implementation. As far as software design inspection is considered, a reasonable assumption is that the requirements specification as input is free of error. Of course, any issues with the requirements specification uncovered during design inspection shall be captured and dealt with. The focus of design reading and inspection is, however, to make sure the design is correct and complete with respect to requirements and the design itself is consistent and clear and has adequate information to start the subsequent detailed design and implementation. Design reading or inspection is crucial since the design quality directly affects the quality of and effort required for the implementation.

6.2   Usage-Based Reading

One of the reasons to read software artifacts is to detect defects early in a development process. However, not all defects have the same impact on end users. Thus the goal of software reading should not be to find as many defects as possible but to find the most critical defects that matter to users. Usage-based reading is developed just for that. A similar idea is employed in the operational profile-based software testing, which greatly improves software reliability (Musa, 1993).

© Yang-Ming Zhu 2016
Y.-M. Zhu, *Software Reading Techniques*, DOI 10.1007/978-1-4842-2346-8_6

6.2.1   Usage-Based Reading Technique

The main idea of usage-based reading is to use prioritized use cases to drive and focus an inspection effort on detecting critical defects that matter most to end users. Use cases are generally developed as specifications of a system. A use case is a set of scenarios together satisfying a common user goal, where a scenario is a sequence of steps describing an interaction between an agent (user) and the software system. Usage-based reading focuses on software quality from a user's perspective. It was suggested by Wohlin and Olsson, and further developed by Thelin et al. (2004).

The usage-based reading is schematically illustrated in Figure 6-1, where the artifact to be read and the list of prioritized use cases are input, and the list of defects are the outcome of the reading. Depending on how many use cases a system supports, prioritization can be done in an ad hoc way or systematically through, e.g., a pairwise comparison using the analytic hierarchy process (Saaty & Vargas, 2001). It is important to note that prioritization shall be done by perspective users or someone who is familiar with the usage of the system.

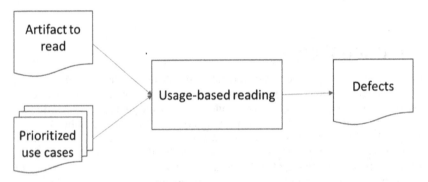

Figure 6-1. *Illustration of the usage-based reading technique*

Two schemes, time-boxed and rank-based, can be employed in usage-based reading. In the time-boxed reading, one allocates a fixed amount of time to the whole reading and divides the allocated time to individual use cases proportionally by their priority weights. Thus an important use case will be allotted more time for a close examination. Alternatively, a rank-based reading can be performed. That is, use cases are examined in their priority order and there is no forced time limit except the whole allocated time. The basic steps of a rank-based reading are listed in Panel 6-1: Instructions for Usage-Based Reading (Rank-Based).

PANEL 6-1: INSTRUCTIONS FOR USAGE-BASED READING (RANK-BASED)

1. Prioritize and sort use cases in order of importance from end users' point of view.

2. Select a use case with the highest priority.

3. Trace and manually execute the use case scenarios through the document under inspection.

4. Ensure the document fulfills the use case goals (the needed functionality is provided, the interfaces are correct, etc.). Identify and report issues found.

5. Select the next use case with the highest priority among the remaining ones and repeat steps 3 and 4, until allocated time is used up or use cases have been exhausted.

Use-case is the common instrument that helps to focus on users' needs. In usage-based reading, prioritized use cases are used to focus the defect detection effort. Use cases are used or involved in other reading techniques as well. For example:

- Perspective-based reading can have a user's perspective, where a reader, who takes the end user's perspective, creates a user's manual or use cases during reading. This is discussed in Chapter 4.

- A reader performs a vertical reading, which is a technique in the traceability-based reading family, and compares design diagrams with use cases to ensure the design is correct and complete. Traceability-based reading is discussed in the next section.

- Use cases are also used in object-oriented (OO) code reading to understand dynamic aspects of an OO system. Use-case-driven reading is discussed in Chapter 7.

The predominant application of usage-based reading is design reading, although it has been applied to requirements documents as well (see the empirical experiences below). It is our opinion that it is a bit awkward to apply usage-based reading to requirements, however. A textual description of requirements is typically developed first, followed by a use-case document. Upstream documents are frequently used to guide the development and review of downstream documents. When used as guidance, upstream documents are assumed to be correct. So employing use cases to guide requirements inspection has a limited value in practice.

Prioritized use cases can be used to direct code reading, e.g., which areas readers focus on and put more effort in. Once a piece of code is selected, a reader tends to have a local view of the code and its functionality implemented, not a global view such as the priority order of use cases. The sheer amount of code in a project is typically much more than an individual can deal with in a reasonable time. It is thus unproductive to apply usage-based reading to code documents. We therefore discuss usage-based reading as a specialized reading technique for design documents.

6.2.2   Variations of Usage-Based Reading

In the usage-based reading developed by Thelin et al. (2004), use case prioritization is performed by an expert of the end system. Winkler et al. (2005), however, suggested that use case prioritization can also be done by readers individually when reading software artifacts, based on one's own understanding of the application domain.

Cantone et al. (2003) reported a use-case-driven reading technique for analysis and design of Unified Modeling Language (UML) diagrams. This is not the same reading technique as that for OO code reading (see Chapter 7), although they have the same name; rather, it is closely related to usage-based reading with the exception that use cases are not prioritized. Analysis and design artifacts under review include a vision document, a use case diagram, a view of participating classes, and sequence diagrams. Four checklists were developed, one for each artifact type, that specify what issues to look for. In addition to checklists, the other idea behind the use-case-driven reading is to specify how to find defects in artifacts ranging from the informal specifications down to use-case realizations and sequence diagrams, using use cases as a guiding light. Their procedure guides a reader to examine the entire set of artifacts, following the order in which they are created using a development process, such as the Rational Unified Process. The authors compared the reading technique with a checklist-based one and concluded that checklist-based reading was more effective. In terms of defect detection rate, checklist-based reading peaked later but at a higher value. The authors indicated that the difference was not statistically significant, however.

6.2.3   Empirical Experiences

Usage-based reading has been tested on design documents in academic settings where subjects were software engineering students (Thelin et al., 2001; 2003; 2004). The effect of use case prioritization in the usage-based reading was assessed first (Thelin et al., 2001). Defects were classified as critical, major, and minor. Thelin et al. reported that readers found different defects using prioritized use cases compared to randomly ordered use cases. Readers who used prioritized use cases detected more critical and major defects than readers who used randomly ordered use cases, and the difference was significant. When all defect categories (i.e., critical, major, and minor) were considered, the difference was not significant anymore, which suggested that prioritized use cases enable readers to detect important defects from the users' point of view. Readers using prioritized use cases were also more efficient, i.e., they detected more defects per hour in areas of all defects, critical defects, and critical and major defects.

Usage-based reading (with prioritized use cases) was compared to checklist-based reading (Thelin et al., 2003). Researchers concluded that usage-based reading was more effective and efficient than a checklist-based one. Readers using usage-based reading detected 75% more critical defects than readers using checklist-based reading, 51% more critical and major defects, but were not significantly more effective in detecting all defects. Readers using usage-based reading detected 35% more total defects per hour than readers using checklist-based reading, 95% more critical defects, and 70% more critical and major defects. Readers using usage-based reading found different and more unique defects, and they started to find defects earlier as well. These findings were confirmed in a replicated experiment (Thelin et al., 2004a).

In their experiment, Thelin et al. (2003) didn't use any active guidance in checklist-based reading. As discussed in Chapter 3, it is possible to incorporate an active guidance in checklist-based reading. Winkler et al. (2005) extended the traditional checklist-based reading by providing an active guidance in design inspection. In particular, readers were instructed to prioritize use cases according to their knowledge of the application domain, and use the prioritized use cases during reading. The difference is that, in usage-based reading, use cases are prioritized by experts. They further compared usage-based reading with the traditional checklist-based reading and its variant with an active guidance and concluded that (1) checklist-based reading with an active guidance was significantly more effective and efficient than the traditional checklist-based reading in finding major defects, and (2) usage-based reading was more effective and efficient than both types of checklist-based reading.

It takes time to develop detailed use cases. Use cases themselves shall be reviewed for accuracy and consistency. Thus use cases shall just have enough details to serve the purpose of usage-based reading. Thelin et al. (2004) set forth to investigate if usage-based reading was still efficient and effective if use cases were prioritized, but without details except only their purposes. Readers were actively developing use cases to fill in more details during reading. Not surprisingly, the researchers reported that reading with full use cases was more efficient and more effective than reading with incomplete use cases. Reading with pre-developed use cases focused readers on detecting defects, while reading with incomplete use cases forced readers to develop a detailed understanding of the documents, enabling them to detect different kinds of defects. Should an organization develop detailed use cases for usage-based reading beforehand or on the fly during reading? Considering the total effort in developing use cases, the authors suggested not to spend time on developing use cases if these use cases are not used in the application development. The authors further suggested a hybrid approach, i.e., develop complete use cases if they are important and develop incomplete use cases if they are less important.

Erlansson et al. (2002) tested usage-based reading on detecting defects in requirements document written in English. They compared usage-based reading to checklist-based reading, using graduate students as subjects. They reported that readers using usage-based reading didn't detect more defects, even though they spent more time on the documents. However, when the severity of defects was considered, usage-based reading detected much fewer minor defects and more moderate defects than checklist-based reading, and to their surprise, checklist-based reading seemed more effective in detecting critical defects. The researchers added that their findings were not conclusive and they attributed the ineffectiveness of usage-based reading on requirements to several factors inherent to their experiments, including lack of training of the subjects. Information-overloading in usage-based reading could be another factor. Certainly readers had to read through more documents such as, in this case, use cases.

6.3 Traceability-Based Reading

Traceability-based reading is a family of reading techniques for inspecting high-level OO design in UML diagrams. The central feature of this family of reading techniques is to trace information between design documents (diagrams and textual descriptions) for design consistency and between design and requirements for design correctness and completeness, thus the name.

6.3.1 Types of Design Defects

Defects in software artifacts can generally be classified as omitted, ambiguous, inconsistent, incorrect, or extraneous information, which is consistent with the defect classification in requirements specification as discussed in defect-based reading. This classification can be tailored to design documents. The types of defects traceability-based reading intended to detect include (Travassos et al., 1999):

1. Omission: concept(s) from the requirements for a system are missing in the design document.

2. Incorrect fact: a design document has a misrepresentation of a concept described in the requirements for a system.

3. Inconsistency: a representation of a concept in one design document is inconsistent with a representation of the same concept in the same or another design document.

4. Ambiguity: a representation of a concept in the design is unclear and could cause a user of the design to misinterpret or misunderstand the meaning of the concept.

5. Extraneous information: the design includes unnecessary information.

6.3.2 High-Level OO Designs Using UML Diagrams

Software design is concerned with the description of real world concepts that are part of the solution for the system envisioned in a requirements specification. High-level design deals with the problem description without considering constraints. That is, it takes functional requirements and maps them to, e.g., UML design diagrams. This allows designers and developers to understand the problem first before attempting a solution. Low-level design deals with possible solutions. Low-level designs, which serve as a model for coding, depend on a high-level design and the non-functional requirements. We shall point out that what Travassos et al. called high-level designs are sometimes referred to as analysis models (Laitenberger et al., 2000).

Object-oriented development is widely practiced in industry nowadays and UML diagrams are frequently used to document OO designs. Multiple UML diagrams are used to capture different views, different levels of abstraction, or different aspects of a system such as static or dynamic behaviors. These diagrams might be drawn at different times by different designers using different viewpoints and abstractions. Consequently, it is hard to guarantee that these diagrams are consistent among themselves and that requirements are correctly and completely captured by these diagrams. It is important to review and inspect high-level designs to ensure developers fully understand the problem before defining a solution as low-level designs (e.g., an activity diagram). It is more difficult and expensive to fix problems in low-level designs or code than fixing them in high-level designs.

6.3.3   Traceability-Based Reading Techniques

Travassos and colleagues (1999; 2002) developed a family of software reading techniques to detect defects in high-level OO designs captured in UML diagrams. They assume that the requirements specification document is available, along with use cases. However, these documents are not subject to review but used to aid the review of the design. Designs are captured in UML diagrams and textual descriptions, including class diagrams, class descriptions, sequence diagrams, and state diagrams.

Traceability-based reading includes seven reading techniques, as shown in Figure 6-2. Each reading technique focuses readers on some aspects of the design. When all reading techniques are combined, a high degree of coverage of the design can be achieved. The seven reading techniques are organized into two groups, horizontal reading and vertical reading. Relevant artifacts (design and/or requirement) are connected by lines with or without arrows and the lines are labeled with numbers 1 through 7. The lines without arrows indicate a horizontal reading (readings 1-4) and the lines with arrows signal a vertical reading (readings 5-7). The dashed line separates lifecycle documents: above the dashed line are requirements description and use cases, which are generated in requirements definition phase; below the dashed line are high-level design artifacts created in the design phase and are subject to review. Each reading technique has a detailed instruction on what to do and where to look for issues. Detected issues are logged as "discrepancy" instead of defect and then the author of the design can decide if it is a defect, since the reader and author/designer may have different ideas about the design.

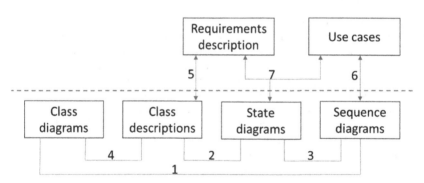

Figure 6-2. *Reading techniques 1 through 7 in the family of traceability-based reading*

To facilitate the understanding of the reading techniques, let's define some key terminologies (Travassos et al., 2002):

- *Functionality*: A functionality describes the behavior of a system from the user's point of view.

- *Service*: A service is an atomic action performed by a system. One or multiple services are used to compose a system functionality. A service can be used in one or more functionalities.

- *Message*: A message is a lowest level behavior. It represents a communication between objects. It is typically shown on sequence diagrams and must be associated with object behaviors. One or more messages are used to compose a service.

- *Condition*: A condition describes what must be true for a particular message to be executed.

- *Constraint*: A nonfunctional constraint such as performance restricts the way a certain system functionality has to be implemented.

Functional requirements describe concepts and services a system has to fulfill. A use case describes important concepts and services a system provides for a user to accomplish a particular task and it typically describes execution paths through the system functionality. A class diagram describes classes of a system and how they are associated (inheritance, uses, composition, etc). A set of class descriptions lists the classes of a system along with their attributes (properties, data members) and behaviors (methods). A state diagram describes internal states of an object and transitions between different states. State transitions are typically annotated with triggers. A sequence diagram describes classes and objects of a system and how they collaborate through sending and receiving messages to accomplish system services.

6.3.3.1   Horizontal Readings

Horizontal readings are designed to check if all of the design artifacts (class diagram, class description, state diagram, and sequence diagram) describe the same system. All diagrams are created in the same design phase, perhaps at different times. The consistency among them is the focus of horizontal reading. Different diagrams contain complementary views to a system. Class diagrams and state diagrams capture the static behavior of the system, while sequence diagrams capture the dynamic one. All views are important, and together they allow developers to understand system behaviors and figure out how to accomplish them. With reading techniques in this group, a reader mostly performs syntactic checking mechanically. There is not much application domain knowledge required. Instead, the reader's development expertise plays a role here.

6.3.3.1.1   Reading 1: Sequence Diagram vs Class Diagrams

The purpose of this horizontal reading is to verify that classes and their relationships captured in a class diagram are consistent with the behaviors captured in a sequence diagram. This reading is thus concerned with the static behavior of a system. To this end, a reader first verifies that classes and objects appearing in sequence diagrams also appear in class diagrams and then verifies that the relationships, behaviors, and conditions in class diagrams capture the services as described in sequence diagrams (Travassos et al., 2002).

Travassos et al. (2002) provided a detailed reading instruction. Here we sketch their main ideas:

- For every sequence diagram, read and understand services the system provides and how these services should be implemented. In particular,

    - identify objects, classes, and actors in the sequence diagram;

    - identify the information exchanged between objects and determine if the information exchange represents messages or services (services are composed by messages); and

    - identify constraints on these messages and services and conditions when a message will be sent.

- Identify and read class diagrams, and determine if the corresponding objects are documented correctly.

    - First verify for every object, class, and actor identified on sequence diagrams, there is a concrete class in a class diagram.

    - Then verify for every service or message identified on sequence diagrams, there is a class on a class diagram, which encapsulates the service or message, and the association between the sending and receiving object is also reflected on a class diagram. Note that in some cases, a reader may need to trace to the parent class of a class. The reader shall also determine if the series of messages is adequate to achieve the intended service.

    - Verify that constraints identified on sequence diagrams can be met based on the information on class diagrams. Those constraints can be the number of objects, permissible values of an attribute, dependencies between objects, timing constraints, etc.

    - Lastly, exercise some professional judgement if the design is sound, with respect to general design principles such as cohesion and decoupling as well as standards and guidelines.

If the reader cannot perform any steps or verify any points above, he or she shall raise a discrepancy. The author of the design will decide if a discrepancy is a defect or not.

6.3.3.1.2   Reading 2: State Diagrams vs Class Descriptions

The purpose of this horizontal reading is to verify that class descriptions capture the functionality specified in state diagrams (Travassos et al., 2002). Thus this reading is related to the static aspects of a system.

Travassos et al. (2002) provided a detailed reading instruction. Here we sketch their main ideas. To perform this reading, a reader starts with state diagrams, and for each state diagram, he or she performs the following steps and verifies the associated points. If any step cannot be performed or any verification fails, the reader raises a discrepancy that will be analyzed by the author of the design.

- Read and understand all possible and permissible states of an object, all actions that trigger state transitions, and how states and actions fit together.

    - Identify the class which the state diagram is for.

    - Start with the start state, trace all transitions and actions to trigger state transitions, and finish at the end state.

- Read and understand the class or class hierarchy for which the state diagram models.

    - On the class description, identify the class or class hierarchy associated with the state diagram.

    - Identify how the class describes and encapsulates states identified from the state diagram above. Encapsulation may be done as an explicit or implicit attribute, a combination of attributes, or a class. If encapsulated as a class type, read the class and class hierarchy. Make sure all states are encapsulated in the same manner.

    - For each transition action identified on the state diagram, verify that there are behaviors to achieve that state transition. Behaviors can be implemented by the class or its parent classes in the inheritance chain. The transition action can be an event or constraint; thus look for an appropriate behavior.

- Make sure the class as described in the class description captures the appropriate functionality, considering the system context and object behaviors and states.

6.3.3.1.3   Reading 3: Sequence Diagrams vs State Diagrams

State diagrams capture the static information and sequence diagrams capture the dynamic information. These different views allow developers to understand the system and objects from complementary viewpoints. However, these differences complicate reading and inspection, since a reader must combine them and identify possible discrepancies. The purpose of this horizontal reading is to verify that every state transition for any object (read from state diagrams) can be achieved by messages sent and received by that object (read from sequence diagrams). Thus this reading is related to dynamic aspects of a system.

Travassos et al. (2002) provided a detailed reading instruction. Here we sketch their main ideas. To perform this reading, a reader starts with state diagrams and reads them one by one. For each state diagram, the reader performs the following steps and verifies the associated points and raises a discrepancy if any step cannot be performed or any verification fails.

- Read and understand state diagrams. The relevant reading steps are the same as those for reading state diagrams in Reading 2.

- Read sequence diagrams and understand how state transitions are achieved via messages sent and received by an object.

  - Identify the relevant sequence diagram(s) in which the object (modeled in the above state diagram) is used.

  - For each of these sequence diagrams, identify services and messages this object receives. On the state diagram, identify the states related to the service and the states leading to and from these states.

  - Map the messages on the sequence diagram to the state transitions on the state diagram. Make sure the mapping makes semantic sense.

  - Look for conditions and constraints of the mapped messages and verify those conditions and constraints are captured consistently on the state diagram.

- Read through all state diagrams to ensure all state transitions are accounted for and have associated messages identified.

  - Identify any state transition on the state diagram that is not yet associated with object messages. If the transition is labeled with a constraint or event, check if there is a message, series of messages, or some action performed by an actor from outside of the system that can achieve the transition action.

When multiple messages are identified on the same sequence diagram for different state transitions of the same object, the reader shall also verify that the ordering of these messages reflects the topological order of the states (the state transition diagram is a directed graph).

6.3.3.1.4   Reading 4: Class Diagrams vs Class Descriptions

The purpose of this horizontal reading is to verify that class descriptions have all the information required by class diagrams and the class as described in class descriptions makes semantic sense (Travassos et al., 2002). Thus this reading is related to static aspects of a system.

Travassos et al. (2002) provided a detailed reading instruction. Here we sketch their main ideas. To perform this reading, a reader starts with class diagrams and reads them one by one. For each class in a class diagram, the reader verifies the following points and raises a discrepancy if any verification fails:

- The class has a class description.

- The name and textual description of the class are meaningful and the description is at the right level of abstraction.

- All attributes along with their types read from the class diagram are listed in and consistent with the class description. The class can encapsulate those attributes, and those attributes are implementable.

- All behaviors and constraints read from the class diagram are present in and consistent with the class description. The class can encapsulate those behaviors, the behaviors are implementable, the constraints make sense for the class and are satisfiable, and the class has a minimal dependencies on other classes.

- The inheritance relationship is included in the class description, if applicable, and the class hierarchy is reasonable (i.e., it is an "is-a" relationship).

- All class relationships (association, aggregation, or composition) are correctly annotated with regard to the multiplicity in the class diagram, the relationships make sense, the correct cardinalities are documented in the class description if important, and the relationship is represented by some class attribute, with a feasible type or data structure. Object roles and responsibilities are documented in the class description as well.

As the last step, the reader goes through all class descriptions and ensures that there is no class that is mentioned in the description but does not appear in any class diagrams. Otherwise this should be reported as a discrepancy, since it represents extraneous information.

6.3.3.2 Vertical Readings

Vertical readings are to check if design artifacts represent the right system as captured in the requirements specification and use cases, which are assumed to be correct for the design purpose. The artifacts involved here come from two different development phases, requirements definition and design. Vertical reading thus prompts readers to trace and compare documents to ensure designs are correct and complete. The artifacts represent different levels of abstraction and contain different levels of details. The design is considered a refinement of the requirements, and there is no single, direct mapping from requirements to the design. Vertical readings are thus complicated and a reader is required to abstract concepts from the design in order to match them in the requirements and use cases.

6.3.3.2.1 Reading 5: Class Descriptions vs Requirements Description

The purpose of this vertical reading is to verify concepts, and services described in the requirements are captured in class descriptions accurately and completely (Travassos et al., 2002). This reading is thus concerned with the static behavior of a system.

A reader starts with the requirements description to understand the functionality, as Travassos et al. (2002) suggested. The reader will then:

- Read through the requirements one by one.

- Identify nouns in the requirement that can be possible classes, objects, or attributes.

- Also identify verbs or descriptions of actions that can be possible services or behaviors in the design.

- Look for conditions, limitations, or constraints on these identified nouns and verbs.

With these identified nouns, verbs, conditions, and constraints, the reader next verifies these concepts are properly captured in class descriptions. For each and every action verb, find a related behavior or combination of behaviors in the class description. For each and every noun, find a related class in the class description. The noun may be used as class name, an instance name of the class, or an attribute name. If a class is matched, make sure its class description has sufficient information related to the concepts, the class encapsulates attributes and behaviors, and the conditions and constraints are described in the class description as well. If a class attribute is matched, make sure a feasible type is used for that attribute.

Lastly, make sure all nouns, verbs, conditions and constraints are reflected and not omitted in class descriptions.

6.3.3.2.2 Reading 6: Sequence Diagrams vs Use Cases

The purpose of this vertical reading is to verify that combinations of objects and messages sent among those objects as captured in sequence diagrams fulfill functionalities described by use cases (Travassos et al., 2002). This reading is related to both static and dynamic aspects of a system.

To achieve the reading purpose, a reader reads and understands use cases first. He or she goes through each use case, identifies the functionality the use case describes, and identifies important system concepts that are necessary to accomplish the functionality. Nouns in the use case describe concepts of the system. For those identified nouns, the reader further identifies verbs that describe actions applied to or by the nouns. Those identified verbs represent services the system provides. Constraints and conditions for those services, if any, shall also be identified. The reader also pays attention to the data or information exchanges in order to perform the actions.

Once having understood use cases, the reader identifies and reads related sequence diagrams, and identifies on these sequence diagrams the corresponding system objects, services, and data or information exchanges that were identified earlier in the use case. A correct set of sequence diagrams must be selected, which relies on deep understanding of the system as well as traceability information. As sequence diagrams are refinement of the use case, the reader may need to identify messages and abstract out the services from these messages.

With these two sets of information identified on use cases and sequence diagrams, the reader next compares them semantically and verifies that they represent the same domain concepts.

- The reader first verifies for every noun identified on the use case, there is a corresponding noun represented on sequence diagrams. For every unmatched noun identified on the sequence diagrams, the reader makes sure it is an attribute of some class by searching through class descriptions; otherwise this could be an extraneous data.

- The reader compares the services identified on sequence diagrams and on the use case. The reader shall focus on the ordering of the messages/services and data exchanged between objects.

- Lastly the reader verifies that the constraints and conditions identified on the use case are observed on sequence diagrams.

While reading and performing the above steps, the reader shall raise a discrepancy if any steps cannot be performed or any point fails the verification.

6.3.3.2.3   Reading 7: State Diagrams vs Requirements Descriptions and Use Cases

The purpose of this vertical reading is to verify that object states and events that trigger state transitions are correct and complete as described in the requirements and use cases (Travassos et al., 2002). This reading is related to the dynamic behavior of a system.

To achieve the reading purpose, for each state diagram, a reader performs the following steps:

- Read the state diagram to understand the object whose states are modelled.

- Read the requirements description, compile a list of states for the object and complete the state adjacency matrix. To complete the task, the reader reads through the requirements description and focuses on where the concept related to the object is described, participates, or is affected. Among those places, the reader abstracts the different states. To identify a state, look for the situations where the object behaves differently as a result of the change of an attribute or a group of attributes. Among all the states identified, determine the start state and end state. Draw an adjacency matrix table, where the row signals a "from" state and the column signals a "to" state. For each pair of states (the order matters), mark if the state transition is allowed with the event and constraints if known or if the transition is forbidden.

- Read use cases and further complete the adjacency matrix. Choose the use case descriptions where the concept is involved. If the state transition is allowed, but the event is missing, complete the event. For the state transitions not determined from the requirements, use the use cases to determine if the transitions are allowed with events or forbidden.

- With those preparations, the reader is ready to examine the state diagram. The reader first checks if all states identified from requirements are represented on the state diagram. Be aware that those corresponding states may have different names. Also be mindful that two states might be merged. Conversely, make sure for every state shown on the state diagram, there is a state identified from the requirements. Once the states from the state diagram and from the requirements are paired, compare the state transitions and their triggers. Again the comparison is a two-way check. Finally, make sure constraints captured in the adjacency matrix are reflected on the state diagram. This is also a two-way check to guard against missing and extraneous constraints.

Like all other traceability-based reading techniques, the reader shall log any discrepancy if any above steps cannot be performed or any verification fails.

6.3.3.3   Semantic Checking

The traceability-based reading family includes seven reading techniques grouped into horizontal reading and vertical reading. In the horizontal reading, a reader compares design diagrams and a textual description. Since those documents represent the same level of abstraction, the comparison is relatively easy and syntactic checking is sufficient most of the time. With tools, the syntactic checking can be automated, which relieves the burdens on readers.

It is the semantic checking that proves to be challenging. This is apparent in the vertical reading group. For example, state names identified from the requirements may not be the same as those directly captured in the state diagrams. Even worse, two or more states can be merged in the design. The reader must understand the requirements and design in order to adequately deal with the situation. As another example, the requirements and use cases talk about system services, but sequence diagrams use messages between objects. In order to properly trace between them, the reader must abstract services out of a group of messages.

The semantic checking is performed or required in the horizontal readings as well, although not as pervasive as in the vertical readings. The aforementioned situation of messages versus services also exists when reading sequence diagrams and state diagrams (in Reading 3, state diagrams use services, but sequence diagrams use messages). In Reading 4, Class Diagrams vs Class Description, the reader is asked to decide if the class description makes semantic sense in terms of encapsulations of attributes and behaviors.

Because of this semantic checking, some level of subjectivity might be involved and a reader's domain experiences play a significant role. That is why Travassos et al. call the detected issues discrepancies, not defects, since the authors may have different ideas or opinions than the reviewer.

6.3.3.4   Practical Considerations

Traceability-based reading defines seven individual reading techniques. For an industrial-scale project, many diagrams may have been created. It is thus a huge effort to conduct a full traceability-based reading. Here we offer a few suggestions to tame the complexity.

If an incremental development process is used in your project, you can review artifacts gradually, as they are created incrementally. If this is not the case for your project, you can subdivide your system into units for inspection. Travassos et al. (1999) offered two alternatives. Each inspection can be focused on some subset of system functionality in requirements or subset of conceptual entities in designs. As the mapping between the functionality and OO concepts is not trivial, there are issues with either approach.

The reading responsibilities can be distributed among team members, to reduce the workload of and to provide focus to individuals. The responsibilities can be divided along the dimension of reading techniques. One possibility is to ask one or more readers to perform the horizontal reading for consistency checking, ask one or more readers to focus on the vertical reading for traceability, and discuss and resolve the discrepancies at the end. The other possibility is to ask one or more readers to focus on static views of a design (i.e., Readings 1, 2, 4, 5) and ask another one or more readers to focus on dynamic views (i.e., Readings 3, 7), with one in common for both static and dynamic views (i.e., Reading 6). The reading responsibilities can also be divided along the dimension of artifacts. For example, reader A can focus on artifacts a, b, and c, while reader B can focus on artifacts x, y, and z. All readers use the seven reading techniques. Of course, the responsibilities can be divided using both reading techniques and artifacts.

If all diagrams and descriptions are available, the development team can use all seven reading techniques defined by traceability-based reading. If some design artifacts do not exist, the team can just skip those reading techniques in which missing artifacts are used. Even if all artifacts exist, the development team can choose and apply a subset of reading techniques, depending on what attributes of the designs are important and what kinds of defects the team wants to detect.

In general, horizontal reading shall be performed before vertical reading, since we want to make sure the designs are consistent before validating them against the requirements. Specific situations may warrant the need to alter the reading order.

6.3.4   Empirical Experiences

Travassos et al. (1999) used undergraduate students to evaluate the feasibility of traceability-based reading. They reported that the reading techniques did allow subjects to detect defects, and a majority of the subjects thought the techniques were helpful. Vertical reading tended to find more defects in types of omission and incorrect facts, while horizontal reading tended to find more defects in types of ambiguity and inconsistency. The research team continued to improve and refine the reading techniques by conducting observational studies and case studies, and the results were summarized in Travassos et al. (2002). The reading techniques could be easily integrated into a development process, they indeed caught critical defects, and the effort was not prohibitively high when compared to other system tasks.

Traceability-based reading was successfully applied in industrial environments. Melo et al. (2001) reported a case study in which the reading techniques were applied in an industrial environment at Oracle Brazil, where a team of five people participated. Reading techniques allowed participants to find, on average, 35 defects (the most was 57 and the least 12). The number of false-positive defects was very low (0.8 on average). The average time spent (individual reading and meeting) was 5.8 hours and the average time per defect was 15 minutes. Conradi et al. (2003) conducted an industrial experiment at Ericsson in Norway. Traceability-based reading techniques were slightly tailored to their environment. They reported that traceability-based reading techniques fit well in an incremental development process, and engineers employing the techniques found more defects (39 vs 25) than their existing reading techniques, which were a mixture of checklists and guidelines, while the cost efficiency was almost the same (1.28 vs 1.37 defects per hour). Traceability-based reading seems to be complementary to their existing reading techniques as they found different types of defects, and engineers employing the new reading techniques found more defects of omission and inconsistency types. However, the new techniques need to be simplified with added questions and special guidelines for their project.

The ideas behind traceability-based reading have been used in other reading techniques. One can clearly see the influence of traceability-based reading in perspective-based reading of design from an analyst's viewpoint (Laitenberger et al., 2000). The architecture reading techniques presented in the next section was also motivated by traceability-based reading.

6.4 Architecture Reading

Software architecture is becoming a mature discipline. It is the blueprint for the software system development and has a far-reaching impact on organizations. Thus it is critical to review and get it right early on (and review it regularly afterward). The principal objectives of architecture reviews are to evaluate if the architecture can potentially deliver a system to fulfill the quality requirements and to identify potential risks. Babar and Gorton (2009) surveyed the current industry practice, and Knodel and Naab (2014) reported their own experiences on assessing industrial software architectures.

Architecting a system is to make fundamental, long-lasting, and hard-to-change decisions. These decisions can be implicit as made in an architect's head or explicit as found in documentation and manifested as implemented in the system (Knodel & Naab, 2014). Architecture review or evaluation is to assess all of these decisions. In this section we discuss architecture reading techniques, i.e., we are only concerned with reading and finding defects in software architecture documentation.

6.4.1 What Is Software Architecture?

Software architecture is a widely used term now. There are many definitions that capture different aspects of software architecture, and there is no commonly accepted definition. We like the definition used by Clements et al. (2011; Bass et al., 2013) : *The software architecture of a system is the set of structures needed to reason about the system, which comprises software elements, relations among them, and properties of both.*

Software architecture is important. Bass et al. (2013) listed many reasons, including inhibiting or enabling a system's quality attributes (-ilities), reasoning about and managing changes, predicting system qualities even before it is built, enhancing communication among stakeholders, carrying early and fundamental design decisions, defining constraints on an implementation, influencing the organizational structure, enabling evolutionary prototyping, improving cost and schedule estimates, supplying a transferable and reusable model, allowing incorporation of independently developed components, restricting the vocabulary of design alternatives, and providing a basis for training.

A software architecture is shaped by many factors, and in turn, the architecture influences these factors. In addition to technique requirements, business, technical, project, and professional contexts influence the architecture (Bass et al., 2013). A software architecture is documented in a software architecture description that is both descriptive and prescriptive. An architecture description typically has textual description decorated with graphical diagrams, capturing module views, component-and-connector views, and allocation views using architecture patterns, styles, and frameworks (Clements et al., 2011).

We shall mention the differences between architecture and design. Architecture is design, but not all designs are architecture. The architecture is concerned with the fundamental structure of the system that delivers the quality attributes. These quality attributes are non-functional requirements and typically referred to as –ilities, such as availability, interoperability, modifiability, performance, security, testability, usability, and so on. High-level design as discussed in the traceability-based reading is a form of requirements analysis and expresses the requirements in analysis models, which are easy for designers to consume. Design is figuring out how to implement the functionalities within the software architecture constraints. Some authors dislike the term "detailed design," as architecture design can occasionally be very detailed in some areas if the architects think they are important.

6.4.2   Traceability-Based Architecture Reading

The general concerns of architecture reading are thus to make sure different views are consistent in addition to complementary, and all views are correct with respect to and traceable to the requirements as well as other architecture drivers. The general ideas behind the traceability-based reading appear to be applicable to architecture reading. Carver and Lemon (2005) developed the architectural reading techniques, which were rightly motivated by the traceability-based reading.

One horizontal reading and three vertical reading techniques are available for traceability-based architecture reading:

- The horizontal reading is to compare the information in one part of the architecture description to the other parts of the architecture description and ensure they are consistent. More specifically, the following pairwise comparisons between views are performed:

    - Logical structures (module views) vs communications patterns (component-and-connector views)

    - Logical structures vs physical structures (allocation views)

    - Communication patterns vs physical structures

- The first vertical reading is to check if the logical decomposition captured in the module views is realistic, judged from the information in the requirements document.

- The second vertical reading is to check if the communication patterns captured in the component-and-connector views are accurate based on the requirements document.

- The third vertical reading is to compare the information about the stakeholders, architectural concerns, and rationale captured in the architecture description to the information in the requirements and ensure they are consistent.

Note that besides the requirements, other architectural drivers are not considered in the initial version of the architecture reading. An excerpt of the first vertical reading (module views vs requirements) is shown here (Carver & Lemon, 2005):

1. Read through the requirements and compile a list of modules that implement the system.

2. For each module view in the architecture document, read through all relevant sections of the architecture document.

   a. For each module in the module view, make sure there is a module identified from requirements in Step 1. If there is no match, log an issue as potentially extraneous information.

   b. Conversely, for each module identified in Step 1, make sure there is a module view in architecture that contains that module. If there is no match, log an issue on potential missing information. If the match is not found in the current module view, decide if that module should have been included in the view.

   c. Use the requirements as the guide to examine the relationship among modules. If the relationship does not make semantic sense (e.g., use relation, is-a relation, part-of relation), log an issue as potential incorrect fact. This also decides whether the existence of a module in the module view makes sense or not, taking into account the intentions of the module view.

6.4.3   Empirical Experiences

Carver and Lemon (2005) conducted a feasibility study of the traceability-based architecture reading and compared it with checklist-based reading, using students as subjects. The checklist was adopted from the first edition of the book by Clements et al. (2011). They concluded that, with checklist-based reading, subjects were more effective at finding defects of commission than defects of omission; with traceability-based architecture reading, subjects were more effective at finding defects of omission than defects of commission. Subjects reported that they preferred traceability-based architecture reading over checklist-based reading, as the former helps readers focus and provides more detailed and structured guidance to read and inspect the whole document set. Traceability-based architecture reading appears to be feasible and easy to understand and use. The authors didn't publish a follow-up study of the reading technique and there was no independent replication yet.

We shall be cautious on the omission defects, however. As the architecture description is meant to document the architecturally significant decisions, the architect may choose to leave some details to downstream designers. In other words, the architect does not care whatsoever how a subpart of the system is designed and constructed. Thus a miss is not really a miss from the architect's point of view. For that reason, readers log potential issues for architects to address.

6.4.4   Other Architecture Reading Techniques

As mentioned earlier, architecture reading is only a small portion of architecture review or evaluation and is concerned with reading and finding defects in architecture documentation. Clements et al. (2011) devoted one chapter to software architecture document review. They presented a six-step procedure, and the fifth step is to perform the review, which is assisted with sets of questions. They defined a template for a question set. Which set of questions to use depends on the purpose of an architecture review. During the lifecycle of a system, the architecture document shall be reviewed often and for different purposes, such as to check if it has captured the right stakeholders and their concerns in the concept phase or to check if it can support development in the development phase. The questions for a purposed review are organized for different stakeholders. For example, software development managers, designers and implementers, integrators, testers, and quality assurance engineers are stakeholders when assessing whether the architecture document can support development. The concerns of these stakeholders are also provided to assist the architecture document review. The styles of the questions are sometimes similar to what one would expect in an active design review. One can clearly see some flavors of checklist-based and perspective-based readings in their approach.

We would be remiss if we didn't mention the state of the practice for software architecture evaluation. Broadly speaking, there are two approaches to software architecture assessment, scenario-based and model-based. The very first architecture review technique is software architecture analysis method (SAAM). The SAAM is a scenario-based method. Here a scenario is a brief description of some anticipated or desired use of a system. Essentially the SAAM develops, classifies, and prioritizes the scenarios and assesses how and if the scenarios can be mapped to the architecture. The method was originally developed to assess an architecture for modifiability and superseded by a new general method, architecture tradeoff analysis method (ATAM). ATAM is applicable to assess almost any quality attribute, particularly the tradeoff among conflicting ones, but it is a very expensive method – it involves a big team for a few days. A lightweight version has recently been proposed by the team at the Software Engineering Institute. Besides the general purpose methods, there are specific ones focusing on particular quality attributes, e.g., architecture-level modifiability analysis (ALMA), performance analysis of software architecture (PASA). On the other hand, the model-based approach uses some formal models that can be automatically analyzed with tools. Architecture description languages are formal languages for describing and analyzing architectures. Interested readers can find more information in books on architecture evaluation, such as Clements et al. (2002).

6.5 Scope-Based Reading

The objectives of software reading are for analysis or for construction. Almost all the reading techniques discussed in this book belong to the category of reading for analysis (defect detection). Here we discuss one reading technique, scope-based reading, of which the purpose is for construction (Shull, 1998; Shull et al. 2000). Reading for construction is useful for software maintenance or new system development from reusable components, frameworks, and architectures. Scope-based reading was developed to enable readers to reuse both the design and implementation of OO application frameworks.

6.5.1 What Is an Application Framework?

An application framework—particularly an OO framework—is a reusable design and implementation of all or part of a system for a specific class of software, represented as a set of cooperating classes, including abstract ones, and the way their instances interact. It provides a skeleton application for a particular domain and regulates interactions among various constituting elements. It typically has a set of hotspots where framework users can extent, customize, or plug in their own components. A framework serves to speed up application development by providing a foundation and a set of design and implementation elements that can be built upon and expanded as required.

From a software engineering perspective, it is desirable to develop an application framework to facilitate software development, since there are many advantages of framework-based development as claimed by proponents of this technology and supported by many successful industrial stories. Although the development of OO frameworks requires significant effort, the benefits generally justify the initial effort.

There are many different kinds of application frameworks. The development of OO application frameworks in general and domain-specific frameworks in particular has been a major industry thrust. There is big body of literature on framework construction, but literature on how to learn and use frameworks is scarce. The very steep learning curve of application framework is notoriously known among software practitioners.

6.5.2 Scope-Based Reading Techniques

Scope-based reading is meant to help developers learn and use white-box OO frameworks. Here white-box means that the internal part of the framework, particularly the class hierarchy, is exposed to the users who typically derive subclasses to implement new functionalities for new applications. As the application domain becomes better understood, the framework becomes mature and it evolves from white-box toward black-box.

There are two effective ways to learn an OO application framework: by studying the class hierarchy of the framework, and by studying example applications. Shull et al. (2000) proposed two corresponding reading techniques: hierarchy-based reading and example-based reading, together known as scope-based reading. These techniques give readers a different scope or breadth of knowledge about the framework, thus the name.

Scope-based reading assumes an OO application framework is given, the reader wants to construct an application making use of the framework, he or she already has the object model and dynamic model of the application to be built, and the object model and dynamic model are not adapted to the application framework yet.

6.5.2.1 Hierarchy-Based Reading

Hierarchy-based reading uses a stepwise approach. To help developers understand the functionality provided by the framework, it concentrates readers on the base or abstract classes first, then moves down the class hierarchy to the derived classes to find the most specific instantiation. It has the following steps (Shull et al., 2000):

1. Study the class hierarchy of the application framework. Determine which part of the framework architecture contains the functionalities that can be used or modified for the application under construction and identify base classes that can be used in the new application.

2. Identify classes related to the new application. For each class in the object model, find an appropriate class in the framework from which the class can be derived, and read and understand the framework class. If an appropriate class is not found, consider aggregating multiple framework classes to create a new class with the required attributes and operations.

3. Revise the object model and dynamic model for the application by using classes from the framework directly or classes composed from multiple framework classes, with details such as relevant attributes and operations.

4. Develop the application using the modified object models by deriving or aggregating framework classes wherever possible to reuse the attributes and operations provided by the framework. Write code as needed to extend the functionality and add new classes as needed to complete the new application.

Hierarchy-based reading has a steep learning curve. The reader has to understand how different pieces of the framework fit together before being productive. In practice, it is almost always supplemented with other reading techniques, such as the example-based reading technique discussed in the next section.

6.5.2.2 Example-Based Reading

The main idea behind the example-based reading is to learn from examples (Shull et al., 2000). It assumes there is a collection of examples, illustrating the range of functionality and behavior provided by the framework. The examples can be provided by framework developers as applets or developed by others as real-world applications. Further assume the reader understands the functionality of the application he or she is constructing. Example-based reading is an iterative process, since the new application will be built incrementally, feature by feature.

1. Decide which functionality should be added to the application under construction in the current increment. Search the collection of examples to find out which example provides the most complete coverage of that functionality. The reader can run each example in turn to check what features were implemented in the example.

2. Study the selected example in depth, but focus on the functionality being sought. By running the example, the reader constructs a set of use cases related to the sought-after functionality. For each use case, the reader traces the code, e.g., in the debug mode, to identify which objects/classes, attributes, and operations/methods are involved and how they cooperate to achieve the functionality. It is necessary to read, understand, and document the relevant code along the way, including the object models and dynamic models related to the use cases.

3. Revise the object model and dynamic model for the application, based on the newly discovered or learned information.

4. Add the functionality to the application. The reader adds new classes modified from the example and augments existing ones with new attributes or methods. If the example does not implement the complete functionality, the reader writes additional code as needed. He or she also provides code to integrate the newly implemented functionality to the application.

5. Go back to Step 1 for the remaining functionalities, if the application is not complete yet.

During the above reading process, it is a good practice to record what is done, what decision is made, and the rationale behind the decision. For example, when selecting one particular example to study in depth, the reader can note which functionality is being sought, what are the candidate examples, and why a particular example is chosen, etc.

Example-based reading can quickly make the reader more productive. However, it is unlikely that the framework originator will or can provide a big set of examples to cover the complete features the framework provides and enables. It is also a concern, at least for a non-trivial application, whether the functionalities borrowed from different examples can coherently coexist in the final, finished application.

6.5.3   Empirical Experiences

Shull (1998) and Shull et al. (2000) used software engineering students as subjects and conducted an exploratory experiment in an academic environment to test the effectiveness of hierarchy-based and example-based techniques. They concluded, in their environment, that example-based techniques are well-suited to use by beginning learners and hierarchy-based techniques are not well-suited to use by beginners under a tight schedule. Example-based learning is a natural way to approach learning of a complicated system. Hierarchy-based technique is time-consuming and does not give developers an idea of where the starting place for implementation is or where they can look for certain functionality. The hierarchy-based technique would have been very effective if there has been sufficient documentation or the developers have been given more time. The example-based technique is not without problems, however. Developers experienced difficulty in finding and extracting a small functionality embedded in much larger examples. The effectiveness of the example-based technique depends on breadth of functionality and other characteristics of example applications. Quite often the rationale of the design choice is missing from examples, which makes it hard for developers to reason about their choice. The example-based technique may limit the developers to explore beyond what examples provide.

6.6 Summary

In addition to generic reading techniques such as ad hoc, checklist-based, and perspective-based reading discussed in earlier chapters, this chapter introduced specific reading techniques for design inspection. Usage-based reading employs prioritized use cases to focus readers' attention on what matters most to end users. Traceability-based reading is applicable to inspecting OO designs. The family includes seven techniques organized as horizontal reading and vertical reading, with the semantic checking as a theme across both. Horizontal reading ensures all design artifacts are consistent among themselves and vertical reading ensures designs are consistent with the requirements specification. Architecture reading is an emerging reading technique, motivated by the ideas behind traceability-based reading. While these reading techniques focus on defect detection in software artifacts such as design and architecture, scope-based reading is meant for developers to read the application framework and figure out how to construct software applications. With these ranges of reading techniques, you are ready to read and understand various software design artifacts to accomplish various tasks, be it for defect detection or for constructions.

6.7 References

(Bass, 2013) L. Bass, P. Clements, and R. Kazman, Software Architecture in Practice, 3rd ed., Addison-Wesley, 2013.

(Babar, 2009) M.A. Babar and I. Gorton, Software architecture review: the state of practice, IEEE Computer, vol.42, no.7, pp.26-32, 2009.

(Cantone, 2003) G. Cantone, L. Colasanti, Z.A. Abdulnabi, A. Lomartire, and G. Calavaro, Evaluating checklist-based and use-case-driven reading techniques as applied to software analysis and design UML artifacts, LNCS 2765, pp.142-165, 2003.

(Carver, 2005) J. Carver and K. Lemon, Architecture reading techniques: a feasibility study, Proceedings of 4th International Symposium on Empirical Software Engineering (late breaking research track), pp.17-20, 2005.

(Clements, 2002) P. Clements, R. Kazman, and M. Klein, Evaluating Software Architectures: Methods and Case Studies, Addison-Wesley, 2002.

(Clements, 2011) P. Clements, F. Bachmann, L. Bass, D. Garlan, J. Ivers, R. Little, P. merson, R. Nord, and J. Stafford, Documenting Software Architectures: Views and Beyond, 2nd ed., Addison-Wesley, 2011.

(Conradi, 2003) R. Conradi, P. Mohagheghi, T. Arif, L.C. Hegde, G.A. Bunde, and A. Pedersen, Object-oriented reading techniques for inspection of UML models – An industrial experiment, Lecture Notes in Computer Science, vol.2743, pp.483-500, 2003.

(Erlansson, 2002) M. Erlansson, T. Thelin, and M. Host, Usage-based reading for inspections of software requirements, 2nd Conference on Software Engineering Research and Practice in Sweden, 2002.

(Knodel, 2014) J. Knodel and M. Naab, Software architecture evaluation in practice – retrospective on more than 50 architecture evaluations in industry, IEEE/IFIP Conference on Software Architecture (WICSA), pp.115-124, 2014.

(Laitenberger, 2000) O. Laitenberger, C. Atkinson, M. Schlich, K. El Emam, An experimental comparison of reading techniques for defect detection in UML design documents, Journal of Systems and Software, vol.53, no.2, pp.183-204, 2000.

(Melo, 2001) W. Melo, F. Shull, and G.H. Travassos, Software review guidelines, Technical Report ES-556/01, Systems Engineering and Computer Science Program, COPPE. Federal University of Rio de Janeiro, 2011 (http://www.cos.ufrj.br/uploadfile/es55601.pdf accessed on March 10, 2016).

(Musa, 1993) J.D. Musa, Operational profiles in software reliability engineering, IEEE Software, vol.10, no.2, pp.14-32, 1993.

(Saaty, 2001) T.L Saaty and L.G. Vargas, Models, Methods, Concepts and Applications of the Analytic Hierarchy Process, Kluwer Acdemic Publishers, 2001.

(Shull, 1998) F. Shull, Developing techniques for using software documents: A series of empirical studies, Ph.D Dissertation, University of Maryland at College Park, MD, 1998.

(Shull, 2000) F. Shull, F. Lanubile, and V.R. Basili, Investigating reading techniques for object-oriented framework learning, IEEE Transactions on Software Engineering, vol.26, no.11, pp.1101-1118, 2000.

(Thelin, 2001) T. Thelin, P. Runeson, and B. Regnell, Usage-based reading – an experiment to guide reviewers with use-cases, Information and Software Technology, vol.43, no.15, pp.925-938, 2001.

(Thelin, 2003) T. Thelin, P. Runeson, and C. Wohlin, An experimental comparison of usage-based ad checklist-based reading, IEEE Transactions on Software Engineering, vol.29, no.8, pp.687-704, 2003.

(Thelin, 2004a) T. Thelin, C. Andersson, P. Runeson, N. Dzamashvili-Fogelstrom, A replicated experiment of usage-based and checklist-based reading, 10th International Symposium on Software Metrics, pp.246-256, 2004.

(Thelin, 2004) T. Thelin, P. Runeson, C. Wohlin, T. Olsson, and C. Andersson, Evaluation of usage-based reading – conclusions after three experiments, Empirical Software Engineering, vol.9, pp.77-110, 2004.

(Travassos, 1999) G.H. Travassos, F. Shull, M. Fredericks, and V.R. Basili, Detecting defects in object-oriented designs: using reading techniques to increase software quality, Proceedings of the 14th ACM SIGPLAN Conference on Object-oriented Programming, Systems, Languages, and Applications, pp.47-56, 1999.

(Travassos, 2002) G.H. Travassos, F. Shull, J. Carver, and V.R. Basili, Reading techniques for OO design inspections, Technical Report CS-TR4353, University of Maryland, 2002 (http://www.cs.umd.edu/projects/SoftEng/ESEG/papers/CS-TR4353.pdf accessed on March 10, 2016).

(Winkler, 2005) D. Winkler, S. Biffl, and B. Thurnher, Investigating the impact of active guidance on design inspection, LNCS 3547, pp.458-473, 2005.

CHAPTER 7

■ ■ ■

Code Reading Techniques

Most of the reading techniques discussed in Chapters 3 and 4 can be applied to code reading. This chapter first emphasizes the importance of code reading as a professional skill and discusses how people actually read code in practice. It then focuses on a few specific reading techniques for programmers to read and comprehend the programming source code. Reading by stepwise abstraction can be used for structured code. Object-oriented (OO) languages such as C++, Java, and C# are very popular nowadays. However, OO code reading is challenging. Stepwise abstraction is extended to support OO reading. To understand both static and dynamic aspects of the OO code, use-cases are used to direct the reading process. Object-oriented framework reading is even more challenging and functionality-based reading is an effective and efficient technique in finding defects in frameworks. Software developers spend most of their professional lives on reading other developers' code and there are many legacy codes that developers are tasked to maintain. Task-directed reading is developed to fill that need. To read and understand the programming code, the readers themselves shall be familiar with the program constructs. This is not covered here, however. We instead cover techniques that are applicable to any high-level programming languages. Lastly, factors that impact code readability are also examined before we conclude the chapter.

7.1 Code Reading As a Professional Skill

7.1.1 Importance of Code Reading

We read programming code for different purposes. As students, we read code in books, magazines, and journals or on the web to learn language constructs and how to master them. As professionals, we may still read code for learning, but most of the time it is for other reasons. We read code written by colleagues as part of the code inspection process; in this case, we read and analyze the code to verify its quality and detect possible defects. We also read code to identify reuse opportunities or figure out how to use it in our own projects. As software developers, a large part of our professional lives is spent maintaining, adapting, correcting, perfecting, and modifying existing code. Empirical data show that developers spend about half of their time on reading and comprehending programs during software maintenance (Maalej et al., 2014). We want to introduce minimal disruption to the existing functionality to maintain its original architectural and stylistic integrity. These purposes are consistent with the schema Basili et al. (1996) categorized, i.e., reading for analysis and reading for construction. To fulfill all these purposes, we must read and achieve a necessary level of understanding of the code. Successful software engineering professionals must learn, cultivate, and master code reading skills.

© Yang-Ming Zhu 2016
Y.-M. Zhu, *Software Reading Techniques*, DOI 10.1007/978-1-4842-2346-8_7

7.1.2   How Do People Read Code?

Program comprehension is an important activity in software engineering and a central activity during software maintenance, evolution and reuse. Comprehension is a process in which individuals build their own mental representation of the program. It has continued to be an active research topic since the 1970s for computer science researchers as well as cognitive psychologists, and there is a rich body of literature in the field. The IEEE Computer Society has been running an annual meeting, the IEEE International Conference on Program Comprehension, since 1992. Von Mayrhauser and Vans (1995) provided a survey of program understanding in 1995. Storey (2005) provided an updated review in 2005 and Schulte et al. (2010) surveyed the topic from the computer science education point of view.

Although program comprehension is a broad topic, much of the research has been focused on code reading and comprehension. Researchers are interested in how people, both experts and novices, read and understand code and what strategies they exploit to facilitate comprehension. Due to its practical importance, program comprehension is still an active and interesting topic today (Maalej et al., 2014).

To understand the empirical findings on how people read and understand programs, researchers put forth numerous, sometimes conflicting, models, which tend to have a set of common elements: an assimilation process, cognitive structures, and the knowledge base (Schulte et al., 2010). The assimilation process is the reading process or strategy the programmer uses to extract information from the code in order to build their mental representation of the code. Such strategies may include top-down and bottom-up. It is similar to the reading techniques we have discussed but less well-structured. The cognitive structure may include a programmer's existing knowledge base on the programming and application domain, and his/her mental representation of the model. Although the elements are common, the views on them are not. It is not our interest here to review and analyze cognitive models, for which interested readers can refer to the aforementioned surveys. We rather summarize the empirical findings related to code reading and comprehension.

Source code is not read like a novel, nor is its meaning determined by seeing how it behaves when run or traced using test data (Deimel & Naveda, 1990). To read and understand the code, one has to build layered abstractions of the code. There are various strategies to build the layered abstractions, one of which is top-down reading. Top-down reading is similar to how we write code. When we write code, we typically follow a divide and conquer approach to decompose a high-level function into multiple low-level ones, recursively as needed. In top-down reading, one gains the understanding of the code by appreciating the overall purpose first, followed by understanding how the function is implemented by constituent components. During this process, the reader repeatedly forms hypotheses about the code, which are subsequently verified, modified, or rejected. The reader scans the code and searches for familiar clues in the text, which are called beacons (Brooks, 1983) or program plans (Soloway & Ehrlich, 1984). For this reading strategy to be effective, one needs to know the overall programming purpose, and well-documented code can usually be read top-down (Linger et al., 1979). This top-down reading approach was theorized by Brooks (1983) and was observed by Soloway and Ehrlich (1984).

Bottom-up reading is the opposite of top-down reading. In bottom-up reading, understanding of the code is accumulated by understanding of small fragments of code. The reader recognizes the function of groups of statements as chunks and combines these chunks to explain increasingly larger program fragments (Shneiderman & Mayer, 1979). Deep knowledge of the programming language and constructs, and of the application domain, helps the reader read and understand the code. Identifying and understanding the control flow and data flow of the program greatly facilitates the global program comprehension (Pennington, 1987). Cross-referencing the program domain and the application domain tends to confirm and enhance the level of understanding, which points to the significant roles the reader's experience and knowledge play during reading and comprehension.

Empirical studies of professional programmers reveal that people do not employ pure top-down or bottom-up strategies but mix them freely (Letovsky, 1987; Littman et al., 1987). Code reading and comprehension is a hard and time-consuming task, and programmers often adopt "as-needed" (opportunistic) approaches to avoid deep understanding (Littman et al., 1987; Maalej et al., 2014). They focus on the task at hand and gain just enough knowledge to complete the task. They do a deep understanding of the code only when they have to. Littman et al. suggested that people adopting the as-needed reading strategy focus on local program behavior and fail to construct successful modifications to the program, since they fail to detect critical interactions among program components and don't have a complete and accurate understanding of the code. The pragmatic approach to code reading and comprehension has also been recently related to code reuse (Holmes & Walker, 2013). Which strategy to use is typically driven by what question the reader is seeking to answer. For example, to answer a "how" question (how a sorting algorithm is implemented), top-down reading is warranted in order to find out the low-level implementation.

Maalej et al. (2014) recently studied the state of the practice of software reading and comprehension. They were interested in the workflows followed by professional developers to read and understand programs, tools they used, and knowledge they needed, accessed, and shared. They observed and surveyed professional software developers at different companies. Their findings confirmed the results of previous studies and revealed some aspects of industry practices. The workflows including reading strategies vary among developers and depend on their skills, experience, personality, tasks at hand, and technology used. The tool usage was very low or limited and some developers were even not aware of the existence of certain features in tools they used daily.

7.2 Reading by Stepwise Abstraction

Reading by stepwise abstraction is a bottom-up reading technique that formulates an abstract description of what a fragment of code does from the fragment itself. It was first presented by Linger et al. (1979), which became the basis for what Basili and Mills (1982) did with greater formality. The reading technique was later integrated into the Cleanroom process, as the verification-based inspection to assert the implementation correctness (Selby et al., 1987; Dyer, 1992).

Linger et al. (1979) have argued that program writing is expanding the known function into a program and program reading is abstracting the known program into a function. When reading code for defect detection, one compares the known functions (design) to their expansions (code). Code reading is thus to recognize directly what the code does or mentally transform it into something that can be recognized directly. The result of this mental transformation is an abstraction, irrespective of all implementation details.

Reading by stepwise abstraction can be applied to reading any programming code. According to Linger et al., a structured program of any size can be read and understood in a completely systematic manner by reading and understanding its hierarchy of prime programs and their abstractions. A prime program is a fragment of code that has one entry and one exit and is irreducible in some sense. The purpose of reading the prime programs is to discover their program functions, and the program functions can be captured as comments in code. A well-structured and documented program can be read top-down, from overall design to lower levels of details. For poorly structured and documented code, however, bottom-up reading is a better strategy, which allows one to discover the intermediate abstractions, successively at higher levels. The process of bottom-up reading is called stepwise abstraction.

The description of reading by stepwise abstraction is not very clear in literature. We can, however, identify the reading instruction in Panel 7-1: Instruction for Stepwise Abstraction.

PANEL 7-1: INSTRUCTION FOR STEPWISE ABSTRACTION

1. Read code line by line to build up a conceptual understanding of code fragments.
2. Connect code fragments to form an overall picture.
3. Compare with specifications to detect defects.
4. Repeat until all code is abstracted and compared with specifications.

Reading by stepwise abstraction can be better understood with the example in Figure 7-1. From code in lines 23-25, one can conclude that b stores the maximum value of the array samples seen so far. Similarly, from code in lines 20-22, a stores the minimum value of the array seen so far. Lines 17 and 18 assign the first element of the array to both a and b, assuming the array is allocated with at least one element. The loop at line 19 loops over the remaining array elements. At the end of the code segment, a holds the minimum value of the array and b holds the maximum value of the array, i.e., a=max(samples()) and b=min(samples()), which is the abstraction one gains after reading this piece of code. Imagine this code segment is part of a larger chunk of code. With reading by stepwise abstraction, that small piece of code can be abstracted as such. Note that the conditional statements inside the loop have a gap (the element value is within a and b, inclusive), and it is appropriate to have an empty operation for the missing condition.

```
17        int a = samples[0];
18        int b = samples[0];
19        for (int i=1; i<samples.Length; i++) {
20            if (samples[i] < a) {
21                a = samples[i];
22            }
23            else if (samples[i] > b) {
24                b = samples[i];
25            }
26        }
```

Figure 7-1. Sample code for reading by stepwise abstraction

Since it was proposed in the 1970s, reading by stepwise abstraction was well studied and compared with other dynamic testing techniques such as functional testing and structural testing (Basili & Selby, 1987; Juristo & Vegas, 2003; Juristo et al., 2012). The general consensus is that the effectiveness of reading by stepwise abstraction varies significantly from code to code, and code reading shall be combined with other dynamic testing techniques in order to detect different kinds of coding defects.

7.3   Object-Oriented Code Reading

In early times, the code reading techniques were proposed mostly for procedural languages. As OO languages and programming techniques became popular, there was a growing collection of evidence suggesting that early code reading techniques couldn't deal with issues with OO programming (Dunsmore et al., 2001). In the following section, we first discuss the challenges raised in OO code reading and then introduce two reading techniques that address the challenges. We conclude our OO code reading with a summary of empirical findings.

7.3.1   Challenges of Object-Oriented Code Reading

OO programming has three hallmarks: encapsulation, inheritance, and polymorphism. These influence how the code is created, structured, and executed. The OO programming paradigm encourages the distribution of functionality related code elements across the system. Understanding of code frequently requires the understanding of code not in the same class, e.g., in its base class or in other composed class. Polymorphism and late binding make the dynamic behavior of the code hard to comprehend. To fully appreciate the code, one needs to understand its static and dynamic behaviors.

107

Soloway and Ehrlich (1984) introduced the concept of programming plan, which is a generic fragment of code that represents typical scenarios in programming. They observed that when a programming plan is distributed non-contiguously in a program, it becomes hard to comprehend since only a part of the code is seen at a time and the reader has to guess based on local information. They called this kind of plan delocalized. This delocalized nature is pervasive in OO programming, and Dunsmore et al. (2001) named the characteristic delocalization. Effective OO code reading has to address this delocalization.

In the following we discuss two reading techniques: abstraction-driven reading, which addresses the delocalization nature of the OO code, and use-case-driven reading, which is intended to address the difference between static and dynamic behaviors in OO systems.

7.3.2   Abstraction-Driven Reading

Dunsmore and colleagues extended the idea of stepwise abstraction to OO code reading, and their systematic reading technique is called abstraction-driven reading. In essence, the reading techniques have the following ingredients, as shown in Panel 7-2: Instruction for Abstraction-Driven Reading.

There are many kinds of dependencies and couplings, such as data dependencies and control dependencies. Dunemore et al. didn't provide details on how to quantify them. Skoglund and Kjellgren (2004) used coupling metrics (interaction coupling, component coupling, and inheritance coupling) to measure and rank the classes and methods so that the reading order can be objectively determined.

When developing the abstraction of a method, the reader should identify any changes of state and outputs in terms of inputs and prior states. The specifications should be brief and complete, describing what the method does but not how. A vigilant reader may have noticed that the abstraction development process is similar to the stepwise abstraction discussed earlier.

Abstraction-driven reading is a systematic approach. It encourages a deep understanding of the code and helps the readers stay focused and on track. The abstract specification generated during reading can be used in future code reading. It is a promising technique to address the delocalization nature of OO code. However, abstraction-driven reading has its shortcomings. It is often slow and time-consuming, and it is not designed to address the dynamic nature of OO software.

PANEL 7-2: INSTRUCTION FOR ABSTRACTION-DRIVEN READING

---

1.   Determine the reading order.
   a.   Analyze the interdependencies and couplings within the whole object-oriented system. Read the classes with the least amount of dependencies first.
   b.   Analyze the methods within classes. Read the methods with the least amount of dependencies first.

2. Read using abstraction.
   a. For each method, reverse-engineer an abstract specification of the method. The method abstract specification may be used to compare with the class specification; it can also be used to support further reading and understanding of other methods (see tracing of referenced methods and classes below).
   b. Trace and understand all referenced classes during reading. This includes reading methods/classes, documentations, previously created abstractions, etc.

7.3.3   Use-Case-Driven Reading

The abstraction-driven reading technique has the potential to discover delocalized defects. To deal with the highly dynamic nature of the OO system behavior, however, additional reading techniques are needed. Use-cases play a significant role in OO system development. For example, they are used to capture the system requirements and play a driving role in the Rational Unified Process (Jacobson et al., 1999). It is natural to use use-cases to guide code reading. We describe use-case-driven reading as originally documented by Dunsmore et al. (2002).

The aim of use-case-driven reading is to check if each and every object behaves correctly in all the possible ways they are used. Specifically, we seek the answers to the following questions: Are correct methods called? Are decisions and state changes made within each method correct and consistent? The reading procedure is described in Panel 7-3: Instruction for Use-Case-Driven Reading.

PANEL 7-3: INSTRUCTION FOR USE-CASE-DRIVEN READING

---

1. For each use-case in turn, devise a set of scenarios that include preconditions, success or failure conditions, and exceptions.
2. For each scenario derived from a use-case:

   a. Document the expected outcome (e.g., state changes, outputs).
   b. Use a sequence diagram or other diagrams that capture the dynamic aspects of the system. Trace the interactions among participating objects that the scenario dictates by following the message calls.
   c. For the class whose code is under reading, verify that the correct methods of the object of that class are called to support the scenario.
   d. Note any decision and state changes in the method of the class under reading and verify that they are correct and consistent with respect to the scenario.

e. When reading the method code, follow the call to other methods if any. If the called method is in the class under reading, follow the method call, read the method and verify its correctness in a similar fashion; otherwise return and follow the sequence diagram.

f. At the end of the scenario tracing, make a note on the final outcomes and compare them to the expected ones. If there is any difference or anomaly, note the location of the difference and mark it as a defect.

In use-case reading, one devises a number of scenarios from a use-case and examines how the classes deal with those scenarios. It forces the readers to consider object behavior in the given concrete contexts, giving the readers a better idea of whether the code is operating as expected. The readers pay attention to missing/incorrect method calls, erroneous state changes, etc. The readers compare the sequence diagram and the implementing code to verify whether the correct method is called in the right context and whether a side effect of the method call is consistent between the code implementation and the sequence diagram, etc. The readers shall also trace other method calls and ensure their correctness. For defect detection, any difference, inconsistency and missing information, as well as its location in code, is noted and analyzed.

It is not feasible to exercise all scenarios and use-cases. Therefore readers take a dynamic slice of the system. In practice, it will detect fewer defects than other reading techniques. Hence, use-case reading is meant to be complementary to other reading methods.

7.3.4   Empirical Experiences

Dunsmore and colleagues (2002) introduced two new reading techniques, abstraction-driven reading and use-case-driven reading, for OO code and compared them to other reading methods, namely ad hoc reading and checklist-based reading. The details of ad hoc reading and checklist-based reading are covered in Chapter 3. To overcome the known shortcomings of the checklist approach, the authors designed their checklist carefully and based their questions off of historical defect. The final checklist includes 18 carefully ordered questions, covering "where to look" (class-level, method-level, and method-overriding issues) and "how to detect" components.

Dunsmore et al. (2001) reported that there is no significant difference between abstraction-based reading and ad hoc reading in terms of number of defects discovered. However, there is a small improvement using abstraction-based reading. Readers using ad hoc reading went through the code two or three times to build up their understanding, while readers using abstraction-based reading read through the code once, at most twice, albeit slowly. Some defects are completely undetected by all readers using ad hoc reading, but this was not the case for readers using abstraction-based reading. That is, abstraction-based reading has the potential to detect delocalized defects. Compared with ad hoc reading, abstraction-based reading also helps readers stay focused and on track.

Dunsmore et al. (2002; 2003) empirically compared the defect detection capabilities of abstraction-driven reading, use-case-driven reading, and checklist-based reading, using experienced students as subjects. They observed that readers using checklist-based reading found more defects and at a quicker rate. However, the detection performance dropped off sharply after the first 60 minutes. The defect detection of abstraction-driven reading and use-case-driven reading appeared to be similar to each other due to a higher initial overhead. Their defect detection performance leveled off at a later time, but not to the same degree. Readers using the use-case-driven method might have discovered more defects if they were given more time. In terms of the number of false-positive defects reported, checklist-based reading reported the most false positives and use-case-driven reading reported the least. These results are not totally unexpected. Abstraction-driven reading is slow and it aims at full understanding of the code. With use-case-driven reading, one has to generate scenarios before comparing the code and the sequence diagram. The researchers reported that although the performance of abstraction-driven reading is not as strong as that of checklist-based reading, abstraction-driven reading appears to be effective at detecting delocalized defects (but less effective at detecting other defects). Use-case-driven reading had the worst performance among the three studied. However, the method deals with the behaviors in the context of executing systems. Among the three reading techniques studied, no single method detected all defects, and there was not much overlap regarding the kinds of defects detected, suggesting a complementary reading approach would work best. This is in line with the underlining idea behind perspective-based reading (see Chapter 4). The combination of these three reading techniques would have the potential to detect recurring defect types (checklist-based), unusual defects that require deeper understanding (abstraction-driven), and particularly defects that are associated with OO programming (abstraction-driven reading and use-case-driven reading).

Skoglund and Kjellgren (2004) independently conducted two experiments to compare the performance of abstraction-driven reading and checklist-based reading. Their experimental results are inconsistent with those reported by Dunsmore et al. Further, Skoglund and Kjellgren reported that abstraction-driven reading gave more support in understanding the code.

7.4 Object-Oriented Framework Code Reading

Object-oriented framework is getting popular. We discussed scope-based reading for OO application construction in Chapter 6. Here we present an OO framework code reading technique for defect detection developed by Abdelnabi et al. (2004), functionality-based reading.

7.4.1 Why Yet Another Object-Oriented Code Reading Technique?

The OO code reading techniques discussed earlier are presumably applicable to OO framework code reading, so why do we need yet another reading technique? Application frameworks are generalized from existing applications in a specific domain. They have light requirements with no specific or fixed set of use-cases. It is not feasible to define all possible use-cases the framework is going to support, since the concrete applications have not been instantiated yet when the application framework is being actively developed. The dynamic behavior of the framework is at least incomplete, since the hotspots will be extended by application developers. Therefore, the OO code reading techniques discussed earlier have only a limited use. Additionally, reading framework involves two aspects: code reading and design reading. The latter is crucial, otherwise a framework with very poor design will seriously limit its potential adoption.

Application framework has a steep learning curve, and understanding the framework remains a challenging task. It is important to understand the structure, both static and dynamic, of the framework when reading the framework code for defect detection. It is thus a wise approach to use the framework understanding to guide framework reading for defect detection.

7.4.2 Functionality-Based Approach to Framework Understanding

Chapter 6 discussed the hierarchy-based and example-based approaches. Similarly, an OO application framework can also be understood by first understanding its top-most framework constructs and then general OO constructs. General OO constructs typically include basic constructs (classes and their relationships, such as inheritance and composition) and advanced constructs (e.g., meta-classes and reflection). The top-most framework constructs include:

- *Components*: Here framework components are fully implemented functionalities that application developers can reuse directly.

- *Interfaces*: Framework interfaces are a collection of abstract operations called hotspots, which are customized and implemented by application developers without altering the structure and behavior of the basic framework.

- *Design patterns:* A design pattern is a reusable, proven solution to a commonly occurring problem within a given context.

- *Framelets:* Framelets are small frameworks that package components, interfaces, and design patterns. They are used to structure and document large and complex frameworks.

To understand a framework, one must extract and understand its functionalities, which can be traced to an operation or a set of operations the framework provides or supports. A functionality can expand to, be implemented by, or use another functionality. Functionalities supported by a framework can be categorized as:

- *Do-functionality:* A do-functionality is a fully implemented capability that every instantiation of the framework application must have.

- *Can-functionality:* A can-functionality is not fully implemented, and application developers must supply their own specific code at those hotspots.

- *Offer-functionality:* An offer-functionality is a fully implemented capability, but its use is not mandatory in an instantiated application.

In the functionality-based approach to framework understanding, one reads the framework code with the intent to extract and abstract framework functionalities, trace them to framework operations (methods), and relate them to other functionalities. In the end, the reader compiles "functionality rules." A functionality rule categorizes a functionality (do-functionality, can-functionality, or offer-functionality), documents the code locations where the functionality is implemented, provides a concise and precise description of the functionality, and lists other functionalities this functionality relates to and the relationship type (use, expand, implemented by). Generating the functionality rules is an additional documentation effort that should happen before code reading takes place.

To develop the functionality rules, one reads the framework documents in a top-down manner, from requirements to designs, and to code as needed. The class source code is read recursively, from the top-most classes in the inheritance hierarchy to the derived ones. The implementation class is read to abstract its function. Overriding methods are read to verify, refine, and update the abstractions established earlier. During reading and tracing, the relationships with other functionalities are established, particularly when an object sends a message to another. Lastly, the functionality is classified as a do-, can-, or offer-functionality.

7.4.3   Functionality-Based Reading

Functionality-based reading is motivated by the framework-based reading and understanding of OO frameworks. Its purpose is to trace the functionality to concrete framework constructs and their associated code. It is a hybrid reading technique: It uses the functionality rules as a guidance (top-down) and reads the code from bottom-up. It has steps as shown in Panel 7-4: Instruction for Functionality-Based Reading (Abdelnabi et al., 2004).

PANEL 7-4: INSTRUCTION FOR FUNCTIONALITY-BASED READING

1. Locate the functionality rules. Arrange for their development if they do not exist.
2. Read the functionality rules in order of categories Do-, Can-, and Offer-functionality.
3. For each functionality rule:

    a. Locate the associated method in the lowest level class; read the code with respect to the description of the functionality, and log any discrepancies as a defect.

    b. Locate the related functionalities. Read them for defect detection, if not already inspected.

7.4.4   Empirical Experiences

Abdelnabi et al. (2004) compared functionality-based reading with checklist-based reading and abstraction-driven reading for defect detection in OO frameworks, using students as subjects. The objects were real and professional C++ OO frameworks, with carefully seeded defects of different types. To make it manageable, subjects were asked to inspect about 1000 lines of code. The researchers concluded that functionality-based reading was significantly more effective (more positive total defects detected) and efficient (more positive defects detected per unit of time) than the other two reading techniques.

7.5   Task-Directed Inspection

There are a lot of legacy software applications around, and software developers are tasked to maintain them. Legacy software code may not be well documented, or the documentation is outdated or simply inaccurate. Quite often it is necessary to continuously improve the software quality of a legacy system, particularly for safety-related and mission-critical systems. Kelly and Shepard (2004) introduced so-called task-directed inspection for legacy code reading. Their main idea was to combine code inspection for defect detection with other software development tasks to reduce the potential resistance to the idea of code inspection, thus "task-directed." They also reported a lightweight process far removed from Fagan-style inspection, which is not discussed here.

Based on the particular circumstances when the reading technique was introduced, Kelly and Shepard defined three tasks, all aligned with the objective to produce useful documentation for the legacy software system:

- **Task 1**. Create a data dictionary for the module. A dictionary is simply a catalog of all variables in the module, including their definitions, units of measurement if appropriate, and the meaning of each discrete value if applicable. The roles of these variables in module calling sequences is also of interest. The reader is to confirm that each usage of the variables is consistent with its definition.

- **Task 2**. Document the logic of the module and add a description as comments in code files.

- **Task 3**. Compile a cross-reference between the code and specifications. Cross-reference tags are created and embedded in both code and specification to signal individual matches. Any mismatches or missing of materials in either the code or specification are recoded.

To accomplish these tasks, a reader will have to read and understand the code, trace the data flow and control flow, and cross-check the code and specification. Since the readers have clear objectives in mind, they are forced to scrutinize the code and related document closely.

Modules are assigned to readers deliberately, considering their background and expertise. All three tasks associated with the same module are assigned to a single reader, taking advantage of the potential synergies between tasks. The three different tasks give the inspectors different viewpoints on the source code. Each reader completes their assigned tasks in parallel, and task-directed reading doesn't dictate any interactions among individual readers, if there are any.

Kelly and Shepard also conducted a case study in the industry environment using professional developers as subjects. According to the authors, 50,000 lines-of-code scientific legacy software was read and 950 findings were recorded. Among all these findings, 6% were considered serious defects and received immediate attention for correction, 56% were related to style and maintenance issues, 33% identified inconsistencies between code and specifications, and the remaining 5% were related to enhanced functionalities. The code was inspected at a rate of 20 lines/hour. At completion, the amount of comments in the code increased from 20% to 60%, which is consistent with the code. The experiment was considered a success and the same technique was applied to other software systems.

7.6   Code Readability Factors

We all know that some articles or books are easy to read and understand, while others are not. We also know that the format of the page can affect reading speed. According to Wikipedia, readability is the ease with which a reader can understand written text, and it can be measured in many different ways.

When it comes to code reading, experience tells us that people read code at different speeds with different levels of understanding. However, we do not have a complete account of what impacts code readability. In the early days of computing programming, researchers kept track of eye motions and focus, trying to figure out how people read code. Based on the observational studies, concrete and sometimes radical changes were proposed regarding code display and formatting (Miara et al., 1983; Oman & Cook, 1990).

There are many factors that can affect code readability. Deimel and Naveda (1990) classify these into five categories. Their classification is still relevant today.

- *Reader characteristics*: A reader's experience and knowledge of programming, programming languages, and application domains play a significant role during code reading and comprehension.

- *Intrinsic factors*: Similar to the intrinsic and accidental complexity of a design, code can have its own intrinsic and accidental complexity, which affects its readability. As we learned earlier, object-oriented programming makes delocalization more prevalent, and delocalized code is harder to read and understand.

- *Representational factors*: Representation factors are broad and can include the programming language, whether the code has adequate and accurate comments, the complexity of the design, the naming conventions for variables and methods, etc.

- *Typographic factors*: Typographic factors include font, color-coding of keywords or other programming entities, usage of white space and indentation, etc.

- *Environmental factors*: Environmental factors are meant to contain anything else, e.g., the lighting in the reading spot, the integrated development environment (IDE), etc.

Numerous books, discussions, and postings on programming styles, standards, or conventions are available. We don't want to start another heated debate here. Rather, we make a few suggestions to improve code readability:

- Pick a coding standard, including formatting and indentation, for the team that most of you agree with. Uniformity and consistency will improve code readability.

- Add comments to the code and keep the comments up to date. Don't document facts obvious from the code. Instead capture the design rationale, assumptions, and decisions as comments.

- Choose your variables, function or method names, and other identifiers carefully and wisely. Make sure the names reflect their intentions. Also make sure the names are consistent with the usage in the application domain.

- Use simple programming structures. Be aware of the KISS (keep it simple, stupid) principle. Stay away from nonstandard language features.

- Add white spaces whenever feasible. Don't clutter the display. Logically group your code.

Different stakeholders will read the code you are writing today, including yourself at a later time. It might be true that the code logic is perfectly clear in your mind at the time of writing. However, you will appreciate your efforts to make the code easier to read if you come back to the code again in a few years, or even a few months.

7.7 Summary

Among all types of software artifacts, source code is probably read, reviewed, or inspected most by different people at different times. People read source code for analysis and for construction. While many of these reading techniques discussed earlier can be used for code reading, we focused on specific ones just for code reading in this chapter. Stepwise abstraction is a classic technique and was developed mostly for procedural programming. As the object-oriented programming paradigm gained popularity, the intrinsic complexity of OO code reading became evident. We discussed the abstraction-driven reading technique, which is meant to deal with the strong delocalization inherent to OO code. To cope with the unpredictable dynamic behavior of an OO system from its static code view, use-case-driven reading can be used as a complement. OO framework code reading is even more challenging, and functionality-based reading is meant to make the reading a bit easier. Legacy software applications are abundant and software developers are often tasked with maintaining and extending them. Task-directed reading can be used to improve code quality and complete the necessary documentation on the code and design. As the empirical and observational studies suggest, in the end, no single reading technique performs best under all conditions. Software developers need to understand the pros and cons of individual reading techniques so that they can call upon different techniques or combine techniques in various ways to fit unique situations.

7.8 References

(Abdelnabi, 2004) Z. Abdelnabi, G. Cantone, M. Ciolkowski, and D. Rombach, Comparing code reading techniques applied to object-oriented software frameworks with regard to effectiveness and defect detection rate, Proceedings of the International Symposium on Empirical Software Engineering, pp.239-248, 2004.

(Basili, 1982) V.R. Basili and H.D. Mills, Understanding and documenting programs, IEEE Trans. Software Engineering, vol.8, no.3, pp.270-283, 1982.

(Basili, 1987) V.R. Basili and R.W. Selby, Comparing the effectiveness of software testing strategies, IEEE Transactions on Software Engineering, vol.13, no.2, pp.1278-1296, 1987.

(Basili, 1996) V. Basili, G. Caldiera, F. Lanubile, and F. Shull, Studies on reading techniques, In Proc. of the Twenty-First Annual Software Engineering Workshop, SEL-96-002, pp.59-65, 1996.

(Brooks, 1983) R. Brooks, Towards a Theory of the Comprehension of Computer Programs, Intl. J. Man-Machine Studies, vol.18, no.6, pp.543-554, 1983.

(Deimel, 1990) L.E. Deimel and J.F. Naveda, Reading computer programs: Instructor's guide and exercises, CMU/SEI-90-EM-3, Carnegie Mellon University, 1990.

(Dunsmore, 2001) A. Dunsmore, M. Roper, and M. Wood, Practical code inspection for object-oriented systems, Proc. of the 1st Workshop on Inspection in Software Engineering, pp.49-57, 2001.

(Dunsmore, 2002) A. Dunsmore, M. Roper, and M. Wood, Further investigations into the development and evaluation of reading techniques for object-oriented code inspection, Proc. of the 24th Int'l Conf. Software Engineering, pp.47-57, 2002.

(Dunsmore, 2003) A. Dunsmore, M. Roper, and M. Wood, Practical code inspection techniques for object-oriented systems: an experimental comparison, IEEE Software, vol.20, no.4, pp.21-29, 2003.

(Dyer, 1992) M. Dyer, Verification-based inspection, Proceedings of the 26th Annual Hawaii International Conference on System Sciences, pp.418-427, 1992.

(Fagan, 1976) M.E. Fagan, Design and code inspections to reduce errors in program development, IBM Systems Journal, vol.15, no.3, pp.182-211, 1976.

(Holmes, 2013) R. Holmes and R.J. Walker, Systematizing pragmatic software reuse, ACM Transactions on Software Engineering and Methodology, vol.21, no.4, Article 20, 2013.

(Jacobson, 1999) I. Jacobson, G. Booch, and J. Rumbaugh, The Unified Software Development Process, Addison-Wesley Professional, 1999.

(Juristo, 2003) N. Juristo and S. Vegas, Functional testing, structural testing, and code reading: what fault type do they each detect? In Empirical Methods and Studies in Software Engineering, vol.2765 of Lecture Notes in Computer Science, pp.208-232, 2003.

(Juristo, 2012) N. Juristo, S. Vegas, M. Solari, S. Abrahao, and I. Ramos, Comparing the effectiveness of equivalence partitioning, branch testing, and code reading by stepwise abstraction applied by subjects, IEEE 5th International Conference on Software Testing, Verification and Validation, pp.330-339, 2012.

(Kelly, 2004) D. Kelly and T. Shepard, Task-directed software inspection, Journal of Systems and Software, vol.73, pp.361-368, 2004.

(Letovsky, 1987) S. Letovsky, Cognitive processes in program comprehension, Journal of Systems and Software, vol.7, no.4, pp.325-339, 1987.

(Linger, 1979) R.C. Linger, H.D. Mills, and B.I. Witt, Structured Programming: Theory and Practice, Addison-Wesley, 1979, chap. 5.

(Littman, 1987) D.C. Littman, J. Pinto, S. Letovsky, and E. Soloway, Mental models and software maintenance, Journal of Systems and Software, vol.7, no.4, pp.341-355, 1987.

(Maalej, 2014) W. Maalej, R. Tiarks, T. Roehm, and R. Koschke, On the comprehension of program comprehension, ACM Transactions on Software Engineering and Methodology, vol.23, no.4, Article 31, 2014.

(Mayrhauser, 1995) A. von Mayrhauser and A.M. Vans, Program comprehension during software maintenance and evolution, IEEE Computer, vol.28, no.8, pp.44-55, 1995.

(Miara, 1983) J.R. Miara, J.A. Musselman, J.A. Navarro, and B. Shneiderman, Program indentation and comprehensibility, Comm. ACM, vol.26, no.11, pp861-867, 1983.

(Oman, 1990) P.W. Oman and C.R. Cook, Typographic style is more than cosmetic, Comm. ACM, vol.33, no.5, pp.506-520, 1990.

(Pennington, 1987) N. Pennington, Stimulus structures and mental representations in expert comprehension of computer programs, Cognitive Psychology, vol.19, pp.295-341, 1987.

(Schulte, 2010) C. Schulte, T. Busjahn, T. Clear, J.H. Paterson, and A. Taherkhani, An introduction to program comprehension from computer science educators, Innovation and Technology in Computer Science Education Working Group Reports ITiCSE-WGR'10, pp.65-86, 2010.

(Selby, 1987) R.W. Selby, V.R. Basili, and F.T. Baker, Cleanroom software development: An empirical evaluation, IEEE Trans. Software Engineering, vol.13, no.9, pp.1027-1037, 1987.

(Shneiderman, 1979) B. Shneiderman and R. Mayer, Syntactic semantic interactions in programmer behavior: A model and experimental results, Intl. J. Comp. & Info. Sciences, vol.8, no.3, pp.219-238, 1979.

(Skoglund, 2004) M. Skoglund and V. Kjellgren, An experimental comparison of the effectiveness and usefulness of inspection techniques for object-oriented programs, Proceedings of the Conference on Empirical Assessment in Software Engineering (EASE'04), Edinburgh, Scotland, 2004.

(Soloway, 1984) E. Soloway and K. Ehrlich, Empirical studies of programming knowledge, IEEE Trans. Software Engineering, vol.10, no.5, pp.595-609, 1984.

(Storey, 2005) M-A. Storey, Theories, methods and tools in programming comprehension: Past, present and future, Proceedings of the 13th International Workshop on Program Comprehension, 2005.

CHAPTER 8

Conclusion

We have explored general and specific reading techniques for software artifacts such as requirements, design, code, and usability. Those techniques are summarized here, with the chapter number where it is introduced. It is a big list. There is no general consensus which reading technique is most effective. We doubt there will ever be for all types of software artifacts in all development contexts. The outcome of software reading is context- and situation-dependent and varies individually.

- *Ad hoc reading (Chapter 3)*. No reading instruction is provided in ad hoc reading and the results strongly depend on an individual's skill and experiences. It can be applied to any software artifacts and is used widely in practice.

- *Checklist-based reading (Chapter 3)*. It can be applied to any software artifacts and is used widely in practice. Checklists are usually artifact-specific and built from historical data or learned from others but customized to project or team's needs. Checklist-based reading enables readers to detect defects covered by the checklist and may limit readers to detect defects not covered by the checklist.

  - As a variant, an active guidance can be provided how to use the checklist. The guidance can also be implicitly embedded in the structure or ordering of checklist items.

- *Differential reading (Chapter 3)*. It can be applied to any artifacts that are changed. Two versions of the document are displayed side by side or in a single view, and changes are highlighted and examined in context.

- *Defect-based reading (Chapter 4)*. In defect-based reading, each reader is given specific steps to discover a particular class of defects. Multiple readers or a review team collectively detect more defects. Defect classes have to be understood and analyzed before specific reading steps can be devised to target specific defect classes. Defect classes are typically software artifact-dependent. In theory defect-based reading can be applied to any software artifact types, but only applications to software requirements were reported.

© Yang-Ming Zhu 2016

Y.-M. Zhu, *Software Reading Techniques*, DOI 10.1007/978-1-4842-2346-8_8

- *Perspective-based reading (Chapter 4)*. In perspective-based reading, each reader reads a software artifact using one specific operational scenario from a particular perspective, and the combination of different and complementary perspectives provides a better coverage of the artifact. It is adaptable to different artifacts and tailorable to organizational or project setting and assigns specific reading responsibilities to readers and provides well-defined reading instructions to focus reading analysis efforts. It has been gaining increased industry adoption in detecting defects in requirements, design, code, and usability. In fact, perspective-based reading includes a family of reading techniques. For a given artifact, key stakeholders shall be identified and then specific reading scenarios shall be developed. For the same stakeholders, different reading scenarios shall be prepared and applied for inspecting different artifact types, since the concerns vary as artifact types vary.

- *Function-point-based reading (Chapter 4)*. Function-point scenarios are alternative to partition software requirements and the scenarios augmented with checklists can be used to focus requirements reading.

- *Combined reading of requirements (Chapter 5)*. Checklist-based reading, defect-based reading, and perspective-based reading have different defect detection capabilities in detecting different classes of defects in requirements. Combined reading takes advantage of the strength of the aforementioned three reading techniques while compensating each other's weaknesses.

- *Test-case-driven reading (Chapter 5)*. Test-case-driven reading employs real testers to screen requirements by writing test cases. The purpose is to inspect the requirements effectively with minimal cost and amortizes the effort across different development phases. It is applicable to organizations with limited resources and can provide good-enough requirements for project decision making early in the software development lifecycle.

- *Usage-based reading (Chapter 6)*. The goal of software reading should not be to find as many defects as possible but to find the most critical defects that matter to users. Usage-based reading is just for that and has been applied to design reading. To do that, use cases prioritized by experts are used to drive and focus design reading. It has a couple variants, e.g., use cases can be prioritized by individual readers themselves.

- *Traceability-based reading (Chapter 6).* This seven-member family of reading is applicable to high-level object-oriented design and documents, and the techniques are organized into horizontal reading and vertical reading. Which reading technique to use depends on the availability of design diagrams and descriptions. As documents may represent different levels of abstractions of the same system, special attention shall be paid to semantic checking, which proves to be challenging. It certainly takes coordination among all readers using different reading techniques on different artifacts.

    - The group of horizontal reading has four reading techniques that trace information between design documents, including diagrams and textual descriptions for design consistency.

    - The group of vertical reading has three reading techniques that trace information between design and requirements for design correctness and completeness.

- *Architecture reading (Chapter 6).* The ideas behind traceability-based reading are applied to architecture reading. Horizontal reading compares module views and component-and-connector views and module views and allocation views to detect any inconsistency. Vertical reading checks the information captured in module views, component-and-connector views, and allocation views to be consistent with requirements.

- *Scope-based reading (Chapter 6).* While all other reading techniques intend to detect defects in software artifacts, scope-based reading intends to aid software construction using object-oriented frameworks.

    - Hierarchy-based reading concentrates readers on class hierarchy in order to learn and use the framework functionalities.

    - Example-based reading is simply motivated by learning from examples. It guides readers through examples in order to reuse or extend functionalities exhibited in examples.

- *Stepwise abstraction (Chapter 7).* This classical technique is for reading any programming code in a bottom-up fashion. It abstracts the programming code recursively and compares the abstraction to the intended specification in order to detect defects.

- *Abstraction-driven reading (Chapter 7)*. This reading technique is applicable to object-oriented code. It builds atop of stepwise abstraction and adds a step to determine the reading order, considering interdependencies among code modules. It copes with the delocalization nature of object-oriented code and focuses on the static code behavior.

- *Use-case-driven reading (Chapter 7)*. While abstraction-driven reading focuses on static behavior, use-case-driven reading emphasizes the dynamic behavior of an object-oriented system. It uses use-cases to slice the software and thus does not provide a complete coverage of code. It works best when use-case-driven reading is utilized as a complementary instrument to other reading techniques.

- *Functionality-based reading (Chapter 7)*. This is intended for object-oriented framework code and design reading. Framework code reading poses a unique challenge as there is no concrete requirement or fixed use case for it – it provides an application skeleton to enable development of other applications. A framework can be understood from the functionalities it provides. And the functionality-based reading combines top-down and bottom-up reading strategies.

- *Task-directed inspection (Chapter 7)*. This is designed to piggyback code review or inspection for defect detection as part of otherwise required tasks that are part of project effort and management mandate. Legacy code is abundant and there is not much documentation (comments and design rationale) for it. Task-directed inspection can be exploited to complete documentation, at the same time improving code quality.

Like design patterns, software reading techniques codify best practices for software review and inspection. Now those techniques are at your disposal. It is expected that those techniques will be tailored to your unique circumstances for their best effectiveness. You could customize, modify, subset, or extend a reading technique, or combine good ideas from multiple reading techniques to create your own. Agile software development has been widely practiced nowadays. Since agile practitioners favor working software over comprehensive documentation, there may be no complete or explicitly written documentation for requirements specification, architecture description, and design. It remains interesting to figure out how reading techniques can be effectively customized and applied in that context.

Software reading is a learned skill. You are encouraged to apply them in order to cultivate your own ability and improve personal effectiveness. You are also encouraged to share with others your experience and lessons learned with those reading techniques.

Index

Get the eBook for only $4.99!

Why limit yourself?

Now you can take the weightless companion with you wherever you go and access your content on your PC, phone, tablet, or reader.

Since you've purchased this print book, we are happy to offer you the eBook for just $4.99.

Convenient and fully searchable, the PDF version enables you to easily find and copy code—or perform examples by quickly toggling between instructions and applications.

To learn more, go to http://www.apress.com/us/shop/companion or contact support@apress.com.

Printed in the United States
By Bookmasters